State of the Union
Addresses of
President Ronald Reagan

with
The Constitution of the United States of America
and Bill of Rights

State of the Union Addresses of President Ronald Reagan

with

The Constitution of the United States of America
and Bill of Rights

First Edition

Bottom of the Hill Publishing
www.BottomoftheHillPublishing.com

ISBN: 978-1-61203-022-7

10 9 8 6 5 4 3 2 1 0

CONTENTS

State of the Union Address
January 26, 1982

Mr. Speaker, Mr. President, distinguished Members of the Congress, honored guests, and fellow citizens:

Today marks my first State of the Union address to you, a constitutional duty as old as our Republic itself.

President Washington began this tradition in 1790 after reminding the Nation that the destiny of self-government and the "preservation of the sacred fire of liberty" is "finally staked on the experiment entrusted to the hands of the American people." For our friends in the press, who place a high premium on accuracy, let me say: I did not actually hear George Washington say that. But it is a matter of historic record.

But from this podium, Winston Churchill asked the free world to stand together against the onslaught of aggression. Franklin Delano Roosevelt spoke of a day of infamy and summoned a nation to arms. Douglas MacArthur made an unforgettable farewell to a country he loved and served so well. Dwight Eisenhower reminded us that peace was purchased only at the price of strength. And John F. Kennedy spoke of the burden and glory that is freedom.

When I visited this Chamber last year as a newcomer to Washington, critical of past policies which I believed had failed, I proposed a new spirit of partnership between this Congress and this administration and between Washington and our State and local governments. In forging this new partnership for America, we could achieve the oldest hopes of our Republic--prosperity for our nation, peace for the world, and the blessings of individual liberty for our children and, someday, for all of humanity.

It's my duty to report to you tonight on the progress that we have made in our relations with other nations, on the foundation we've carefully laid for our economic recovery, and finally, on a bold and spirited initiative that I believe can change the face of American government and make it again the servant of the people.

Seldom have the stakes been higher for America. What we do and say here will make all the difference to autoworkers in Detroit, lumberjacks in the Northwest, steelworkers in Steubenville who are in the unemployment lines; to black teenagers in Newark and Chicago; to hard-pressed farmers and small businessmen; and to millions of everyday Americans who harbor the simple wish of a safe and financially secure future for their children. To understand the state of the Union, we must look not only at where we are and where we're going but where we've been. The situation at this time last year was truly ominous.

The last decade has seen a series of recessions. There was a recession in 1970, in 1974, and again in the spring of 1980. Each time, unemployment increased and inflation soon turned up again. We coined the word "stagflation" to describe this.

Government's response to these recessions was to pump up the money supply and increase spending. In the last 6 months of 1980, as an example, the money supply increased at the fastest rate in postwar history--13 percent. Inflation remained in double digits, and government spending increased at an annual rate of 17 percent. Interest rates reached a staggering 21.5 percent. There were 8 million unemployed.

Late in 1981 we sank into the present recession, largely because continued high interest rates hurt the auto industry and construction. And there was a drop in productivity, and the already high unemployment increased.

This time, however, things are different. We have an economic program in place, completely different from the artificial quick fixes of the past. It calls for a reduction of the rate of increase in government spending, and already that rate has been cut nearly in half. But reduced spending the first and smallest phase of a 3-year tax rate reduction designed to stimulate the economy and create jobs. Already interest rates are down to 15 3/4 percent, but they must still go lower. Inflation is down from 12.4 percent to 8.9, and for the month of December it was running at an annualized rate of 5.2 percent. If we had not acted as we did, things would be far worse for all Americans than they are today. Inflation, taxes, and interest rates would all be higher.

A year ago, Americans' faith in their governmental process was steadily declining. Six out of 10 Americans were saying they were pessimistic about their future. A new kind of defeatism was heard. Some said our domestic problems were uncontrollable, that we had to learn to live with this seemingly endless cycle of high inflation and high unemployment.

There were also pessimistic predictions about the relationship between our administration and this Congress. It was said we could never work together. Well, those predictions were wrong. The record is clear, and I believe that history will remember this as an era of American renewal, remember this administration as an administration of change, and remember this Congress as a Congress of destiny.

Together, we not only cut the increase in government spending nearly in half, we brought about the largest tax reductions and the most sweeping changes in our tax structure since the beginning of this century. And because we indexed future taxes to the rate of inflation, we took away government's built-in profit on inflation and its hidden incentive to grow larger at the expense of American workers.-

Together, after 50 years of taking power away from the hands of the people in their States and local communities, we have started returning power and resources to them.

Together, we have cut the growth of new Federal regulations nearly in half. In 1981 there were 23,000 fewer pages in the Federal Register, which lists new regulations, than there were in 1980. By deregulating oil we've come closer to achieving energy independence and helped bring down the cost of gasoline and heating fuel.

Together, we have created an effective Federal strike force to combat waste and fraud in government. In just 6 months it has saved the taxpayers more than $2 billion, and it's only getting started.

Together we've begun to mobilize the private sector, not to duplicate wasteful and discredited government programs, but to bring thousands of Americans into a volunteer effort to help solve many of America's social problems.

Together we've begun to restore that margin of military safety that ensures peace. Our country's uniform is being worn once again with pride.

Together we have made a New Beginning, but we have only begun.

No one pretends that the way ahead will be easy. In my Inaugural Address last year, I warned that the "ills we suffer have come upon us over several decades. They will not go away in days, weeks, or months, but they will go away . . . because we as Americans have the capacity now, as we've had it in the past, to do whatever needs to be done to preserve this last and greatest bastion of freedom." '

The economy will face difficult moments in the months ahead. But the program for economic recovery that is in place will pull the economy out of its slump and put us on the road to prosperity and stable growth by the latter half of this year. And that is why I can report to you tonight that in the near future the state of the Union and the economy will be better--much better--if we summon the strength to continue on the course that we've charted.

And so, the question: If the fundamentals are in place, what now? Well, two things. First, we must understand what's happening at the moment to the economy. Our current problems are not the product of the recovery program that's only just now getting underway, as some would have you believe; they are the inheritance of decades of tax and tax and spend and spend.

Second, because our economic problems are deeply rooted and will not respond to quick political fixes, we must stick to our carefully integrated plan for recovery. That plan is based on four commonsense fundamentals: continued reduction of the growth in Federal spending; preserving the individual and business tax reductions that will stimulate saving and investment; removing unnecessary Federal regulations to spark productivity; and maintaining a healthy dollar and a stable monetary policy, the latter a responsibility of the Federal Reserve System.

The only alternative being offered to this economic program is a return to the policies that gave us a trillion-dollar debt, runaway inflation, runaway interest rates and unemployment. The doubters would have us turn back the clock with tax increases that would offset the personal tax rate reductions already passed by this Congress. Raise present taxes to cut future deficits, they tell us. Well, I don't believe we should buy that argument.

There are too many imponderables for anyone to predict deficits or surpluses several years ahead with any degree of accuracy. The budget in place, when I took office, had been projected as balanced. It turned out to have one of the biggest deficits in history. Another example of the imponderables that can make deficit projections highly questionable--a change of only one percentage point in unemployment can alter a deficit up or down by some $25 billion.

As it now stands, our forecast, which we're required by law to make, will show major deficits starting at less than a hundred billion dollars and declining, but still too high. More important, we're making progress with the three keys to reducing deficits: economic growth, lower interest rates, and spending control. The policies we have in place will reduce the deficit steadily, surely, and in time, completely.

Higher taxes would not mean lower deficits. If they did, how would we explain that tax revenues more than doubled just since 1976; yet in that same 6-year period we ran the largest series of deficits in our history. In 1980 tax revenues increased by $54 billion, and in 1980 we had one of our all-time biggest deficits. Raising taxes won't balance the budget; it will encourage more government spending and less private investment. Raising taxes will slow economic growth, reduce production, and destroy future jobs, making it more difficult for those without jobs to find them and more likely that those who now have jobs could lose them. So, I will not ask you to try to balance the budget on the backs of the American taxpayers.

I will seek no tax increases this year, and I have no intention of retreating from our basic program of tax relief. I promise to bring the American people--to bring their tax rates down and to keep them down, to provide them incentives to rebuild our economy, to save, to invest in America's future. I will stand by my word. Tonight I'm urging the American people: Seize these new opportunities to produce, to save, to invest, and together we'll make this economy a mighty engine of freedom, hope, and prosperity again.

Now, the budget deficit this year will exceed our earlier expectations. The recession did that. It lowered revenues and increased costs. To some extent, we're also victims of our own success. We've brought inflation down faster than we thought we could, and in doing this, we've deprived government of those hidden revenues that occur when inflation pushes people into higher income tax brackets. And the continued high interest rates last year cost the government about $5 billion more than anticipated.

We must cut out more nonessential government spending and rout out more waste, and we will continue our efforts to reduce the number of employees in the Federal work force by 75,000.

The budget plan I submit to you on February 8th will realize major savings by dismantling the Departments of Energy and Education and by eliminating ineffective subsidies for business. We'll continue to redirect our resources to our two highest budget priorities--a strong national defense to keep America free and at peace and a reliable safety net of social programs for those who have contributed and those who are in need.

Contrary to some of the wild charges you may have heard, this administration has not and will not turn its back on America's elderly or America's poor. Under the new budget, funding for social insurance programs will be more than double the amount spent only 6 years ago. But it would be foolish to pretend that these or any programs cannot be made more efficient and economical.

The entitlement programs that make up our safety net for the truly needy have worthy goals and many deserving recipients. We will protect them. But there's only one way to see to it that these programs really help those whom they were designed to help. And that is to bring their spiraling costs under control.

Today we face the absurd situation of a Federal budget with three-quarters of its expenditures routinely referred to as "uncontrollable." And a large part of this goes to entitlement programs.

Committee after committee of this Congress has heard witness after witness describe many of these programs as poorly administered and rife with waste and fraud. Virtually every American who shops in a local supermarket is aware of the daily abuses that take place in the food stamp program, which has grown by 16,000 percent in the last 15 years. Another example is Medicare and Medicaid--programs with worthy goals but whose costs have increased from 11.2 billion to almost 60 billion, more than 5 times as much, in just 10 years.

Waste and fraud are serious problems. Back in 1980 Federal investigators testified before one of your committees that "corruption has permeated virtually every area of the Medicare and Medicaid health care industry." One official said many of the people who are cheating the system were "very confident that nothing was going to happen to them." Well, something is going to happen. Not only the taxpayers are defrauded; the people with real dependency on these programs are deprived of what they need, because available resources are going not to the needy, but to the greedy.

The time has come to control the uncontrollable. In August we made a start. I signed a bill to reduce the growth of these programs by $44 billion over the next 3 years while at the same time preserving essential services for the truly needy. Shortly you will receive from me a message on further reforms we intend to install--some new, but others long recommended by your own congressional committees. I ask you to help make these savings for the American taxpayer.

The savings we propose in entitlement programs will total some $63 billion over 4 Years and will, without affecting social t security, go a long way toward bringing Federal spending under control.

But don't be fooled by those who proclaim that spending cuts will deprive the elderly, the needy, and the helpless. The. Federal Government will still subsidize 95 million meals every day. That's one out of seven of all the meals served in America. Head Start, senior nutrition programs, and child welfare programs will not be cut from the levels we proposed last year. More than one-half billion dollars has been proposed for minority business assistance. And research at the National Institute of Health will be increased by over $100 million. While meeting all these needs, we intend to plug unwarranted tax loopholes and strengthen the law which requires all large corporations to pay a minimum tax.

I am confident the economic program we've put into operation will protect the needy while it triggers a recovery that will benefit all Americans. It will stimulate the economy, result in increased savings and provide capital for expansion, mortgages for homebuilding, and jobs for the unemployed.

Now that the essentials of that program are in place, our next major undertaking must be a program--just as bold, just as innovative--to make government again accountable to the people, to make our system of federalism work again.

Our citizens feel they've lost control of even the most basic decisions made about the essential services of government, such as schools, welfare, roads, and even garbage collection. And they're right. A maze of interlocking jurisdictions and levels of government confronts average citizens in trying to solve even the simplest of problems. They don't know where to turn for answers, who to hold accountable, who to praise, who to blame, who to vote for or against. The main reason for this is the overpowering growth of Federal grants-in-aid programs during the past few decades.

In 1960 the Federal Government had 132 categorical grant programs, costing $7 billion. When I took office, there were approximately 500, costing nearly a hundred billion dollars--13 programs for energy, 36 for pollution control, 66 for social services, 90 for education. And here in the Congress, it takes at least 166 committees just to try to keep track of them.

You know and I know that neither the President nor the Congress can properly oversee this jungle of grants-in-aid; indeed, the growth of these grants has led to the distortion in the vital functions of government. As one Democratic Governor put it recently: The National Government should be worrying about "arms control, not potholes."

The growth in these Federal programs has--in the words of one intergovernmental commission--made the Federal Government "more pervasive, more intrusive, more unmanageable, more ineffective and costly, and above all, more (un) accountable." Let's solve this problem with a single, bold stroke: the return of some $47 billion in Federal programs to State and local government, together with the means to finance them and a transition period of nearly 10 years to avoid unnecessary disruption.

I will shortly send this Congress a message describing this program. I want to emphasize, however, that its full details will have been worked out only after close consultation with congressional, State, and local officials.

Starting in fiscal 1984, the Federal Government will assume full responsibility for the cost of the rapidly growing

Medicaid program to go along with its existing responsibility for Medicare. As part of a financially equal swap, the States will simultaneously take full responsibility for Aid to Families with Dependent Children and food stamps. This will make welfare less costly and more responsive to genuine need, because it'll be designed and administered closer to the grass roots and the people it serves.

In 1984 the Federal Government will apply the full proceeds from certain excise taxes to a grass roots trust fund that will belong in fair shares to the 50 States. The total amount flowing into this fund will be $28 billion a year. Over the next 4 years the States can use this money in either of two ways. If they want to continue receiving Federal grants in such areas as transportation, education, and social services, they can use their trust fund money to pay for the grants. Or to the extent they choose to forgo the Federal grant programs, they can use their trust fund money on their own for those or other purposes. There will be a mandatory pass-through of part of these funds to local governments.

By 1988 the States will be in complete control of over 40 Federal grant programs. The trust fund will start to phase out, eventually to disappear, and the excise taxes will be turned over to the States. They can then preserve, lower, or raise taxes on their own and fund and manage these programs as they see fit.

In a single stroke we will be accomplishing a realignment that will end cumbersome administration and spiraling costs at the Federal level while we ensure these programs will be more responsive to both the people they're meant to help and the people who pay for them.

Hand in hand with this program to strengthen the discretion and flexibility of State and local governments, we're proposing legislation for an experimental effort to improve and develop our depressed urban areas in the 1980's and '90's. This legislation will permit States and localities to apply to the Federal Government for designation as urban enterprise zones. A broad range of special economic incentives in the zones will help attract new business, new jobs, new opportunity to America's inner cities and rural towns. Some will say our mission is to save free enterprise. Well, I say we must free enterprise so that together we can save America.

Some will also say our States and local communities are not up to the challenge of a new and creative partnership. Well, that might have been true 20 years ago before reforms like reapportionment and the Voting Rights Act, the 10-year extension of which I strongly support. It's no longer true today. This administration has faith in State and local governments and the constitutional balance envisioned by the Founding Fathers. We also believe in the integrity, decency, and sound, good sense of grass roots Americans.

Our faith in the American people is reflected in another major endeavor. Our private sector initiatives task force is seeking out successful community models of school, church, business, union, foundation, and civic programs that help community needs. Such groups are almost invariably far more efficient than government in running social programs.

We're not asking them to replace discarded and often discredited government programs dollar for dollar, service for service. We just want to help them perform the good works they choose and help others to profit by their example. Three hundred and eighty-five thousand corporations and private organizations are already working on social programs ranging from drug rehabilitation to job training, and thousands more Americans have written us asking how they can help. The volunteer spirit is still alive and well in America.

Our nation's long journey towards civil rights for all our citizens---once a source of discord, now a source of pride--must continue with no backsliding or slowing down. We must and shall see that those basic laws that guarantee equal rights are preserved and, when necessary, strengthened.

Our concern for equal rights for women is firm and unshakable. We launched a new Task Force on Legal Equity for Women and a Fifty States Project that will examine State laws for discriminatory language. And for the first time in our history, a woman sits on the highest court in the land.

So, too, the problem of crime--one as real and deadly serious as any in America today. It demands that we seek transformation of our legal system, which overly protects the rights of criminals while it leaves society and the innocent victims of crime without justice.

We look forward to the enactment of a responsible clean air act to increase jobs while continuing to improve the quality of our air. We're encouraged by the bipartisan initiative of the House and are hopeful of further progress as the Senate continues its deliberations.

So far, I've concentrated largely, now, on domestic matters. To view the state of the Union in perspective, we must not ignore the rest of the world. There isn't time tonight for a lengthy treatment of social--or foreign policy, I should say, a subject I intend to address in detail in the near future. A few words, however, are in order on the progress we've made over the past year, reestablishing respect for our nation around the globe and some of the challenges and goals that we will approach in the year ahead.

At Ottawa and Cancun, I met with leaders of the major industrial powers and developing nations. Now, some of those I met with were a little surprised that I didn't apologize for America's wealth. Instead, I spoke of the strength of the free marketplace system and how that system could help them realize their aspirations for economic development and political freedom. I believe lasting friendships were made, and the foundation was laid for future cooperation.

In the vital region of the Caribbean Basin, we're developing a program of aid, trade, and investment incentives to promote self-sustaining growth and a better, more secure life for our neighbors to the south. Toward those who would export terrorism and subversion in the Caribbean and elsewhere, especially Cuba and Libya, we will act with firmness.

Our foreign policy is a policy of strength, fairness, and balance. By restoring America's military credibility, by pursuing peace at the negotiating table wherever both sides are willing to sit down in good faith, and by regaining the respect of America's allies and adversaries alike, we have strengthened our country's position as a force for peace and progress in the world.

When action is called for, we're taking it. Our sanctions against the military dictatorship that has attempted to crush human rights in Poland--and against the Soviet regime behind that military dictatorship-clearly demonstrated to the world that America will not conduct "business as usual" with the forces of oppression. If the events in Poland continue to deteriorate, further measures will follow.

Now, let me also note that private American groups have taken the lead in making January 30th a day of solidarity with the people of Poland. So, too, the European Parliament has called for March 21st to be an international day of support for Afghanistan. Well, I urge all peace-loving peoples to join together on those days, to raise their voices, to speak and pray for freedom.

Meanwhile, we're working for reduction of arms and military activities, as I announced in my address to the Nation last November 18th. We have proposed to the Soviet Union a far-reaching agenda for mutual reduction of military forces and have already initiated negotiations with them in Geneva on intermediate-range nuclear forces. In those talks it is essential that we negotiate from a position of strength. There must be a real incentive for the Soviets to take these talks seriously. This requires that we rebuild our defenses.

In the last decade, while we sought the moderation of Soviet power through a process of restraint and accommodation, the Soviets engaged in an unrelenting buildup of their military forces. The protection of our national security has required that we undertake a substantial program to enhance our military forces.

We have not neglected to strengthen our traditional alliances in Europe and Asia, or to develop key relationships with our partners in the Middle East and other countries. Building a more peaceful world requires a sound strategy and the national resolve to back it up. When radical forces threaten our friends, when economic misfortune creates conditions of instability, when strategically vital parts of the world fall under the shadow of Soviet power, our response can make the difference between peaceful change or disorder and violence. That's why we've laid such stress not only on our own defense but on our vital foreign assistance program. Your recent passage of the Foreign Assistance Act sent a signal to the world that America will not shrink from making the investments necessary for both peace and security. Our foreign policy must be rooted in realism, not naivete or self-delusion.

A recognition of what the Soviet empire is about is the starting point. Winston Churchill, in negotiating with the Soviets, observed that they respect only strength and resolve in their dealings with other nations. That's why we've moved to reconstruct our national defenses. We intend to keep the peace. We will also keep our freedom.

We have made pledges of a new frankness in our public statements and worldwide broadcasts. In the face of a climate of falsehood and misinformation, we've promised the world a season of truth--the truth of our great civilized ideas: individual liberty, representative government, the rule of law under God. We've never needed walls or minefields or barbed wire to keep our people in. Nor do we declare martial law to keep our people from voting for the kind of government they want.

Yes, we have our problems; yes, we're in a time of recession. And it's true, there's no quick fix, as I said, to instantly end the tragic pain of unemployment. But we will end it. The process has already begun, and we'll see its effect as the year goes on.

We speak with pride and admiration of that little band of Americans who overcame insuperable odds to set this nation on course 200 years ago. But our glory didn't end with them. Americans ever since have emulated their deeds.

We don't have to turn to our history books for heroes.

They're all around us. One who sits among you here tonight epitomized that heroism at the end of the longest imprisonment ever inflicted on men of our Armed Forces. Who will ever forget that night when we waited for television to bring us the scene of that first plane landing at Clark Field in the Philippines, bringing our POW's home? The plane door opened and Jeremiah Denton came slowly down the ramp. He caught sight of our flag, saluted it, said, "God bless America," and then thanked us for bringing him home.

Just 2 weeks ago, in the midst of a terrible tragedy on the Potomac, we saw again the spirit of American heroism at its finest--the heroism of dedicated rescue workers saving crash victims from icy waters. And we saw the heroism of one of our young government employees, Lenny Skutnik, who, when he saw a woman lose her grip on the helicopter line, dived into the water and dragged her to safety.

And then there are countless, quiet, everyday heroes of American who sacrifice long and hard so their children will know a better life than they've known; church and civic volunteers who help to feed, clothe, nurse, and teach the needy; millions who've made our nation and our nation's destiny so very special-unsung heroes who may not have realized their own dreams themselves but then who reinvest those dreams in their children. Don't let anyone tell you that America's best days are behind her, that the American spirit has been vanquished. We've seen it triumph too often in our lives to stop believing in it now.

A hundred and twenty years ago, the greatest of all our Presidents delivered his second State of the Union message in this Chamber. "We cannot escape history," Abraham Lincoln warned. "We of this Congress and this administration will be remembered in spite of ourselves." The "trial through which we pass will light us down, in honor or dishonor, to the latest (last) generation."

Well, that President and that Congress did not fail the American people. Together they weathered the storm and preserved the Union. Let it be said of us that we, too, did not fail; that we, too, worked together to bring America through difficult times. Let us so conduct ourselves that two centuries from now, another Congress and another President, meeting in this Chamber as we are meeting, will speak of us with pride, saying that we met the test and preserved for them in their day the sacred flame of liberty--this last, best hope of man on Earth.

God bless you, and thank you.

NOTE: The President spoke at 9 p.m. in the House Chamber at the Capitol. He was introduced by Thomas P. O'Neill, Jr., Speaker of the House of Representatives. The address was broadcast live on nationwide radio and television.

State of the Union Address
January 25, 1983

Mr. Speaker, Mr. President, distinguished Members of the Congress, honored guests, and fellow citizens:

This solemn occasion marks the 196th time that a President of the United States has reported on the State of the Union since George Washington first did so in 1790. That's a lot of reports, but there's no shortage of new things to say about the State of the Union. The very key to our success has been our ability, foremost among nations, to preserve our lasting values by making change work for us rather than against us.

I would like to talk with you this evening about what we can do together--not as Republicans and Democrats, but as Americans-to make tomorrow's America happy and prosperous at home, strong and respected abroad, and at peace in the world.

As we gather here tonight, the state of our Union is strong, but our economy is troubled. For too many of our fellow citizens-farmers, steel and auto workers, lumbermen, black teenagers, working mothers-this is a painful period. We must all do everything in our power to bring their ordeal to an end. It has fallen to us, in our time, to undo damage that was a long time in the making, and to begin the hard but necessary task of building a better future for ourselves and our children.

We have a long way to go, but thanks to the courage, patience, and strength of our people, America is on the mend.

But let me give you just one important reason why I believe this--it involves many members of this body.

Just 10 days ago, after months of debate and deadlock, the bipartisan Commission on Social Security accomplished the seemingly impossible. Social security, as some of us had warned for so long, faced disaster. I, myself, have been talking about this problem for almost 30 years. As 1983 began, the system stood on the brink of bankruptcy, a double victim of our economic ills. First, a decade of rampant inflation drained its reserves as we tried to protect beneficiaries from the spiraling cost of living. Then the recession and the sudden end of inflation withered the expanding wage base and increasing revenues the system needs to support the 36 million Americans who depend on it.

When the Speaker of the House, the Senate majority leader, and I performed the bipartisan--or formed the bipartisan Commission on Social Security, pundits and experts predicted that party divisions and conflicting interests would prevent the Commission from agreeing on a plan to save social security. Well, sometimes, even here in Washington, the cynics are wrong. Through compromise and cooperation, the members of the Commission overcame their differences and achieved a fair, workable plan. They proved that, when it comes to the national welfare, Americans can still pull together for the common good.

Tonight, I'm especially pleased to join with the Speaker and the Senate majority leader in urging the Congress to enact this plan by Easter.

There are elements in it, of course, that none of us prefers, but taken together it performs a package that all of us can support. It asks for some sacrifice by all--the self-employed, beneficiaries, workers, government employees, and the better-off among the retired--but it imposes an undue burden on none. And, in supporting it, we keep an important pledge to the American people: The integrity of the social security system will be preserved, and no one's payments will be reduced.

The Commission's plan will do the job; indeed, it must do the job. We owe it to today's older Americans and today's younger workers. So, before we go any further, I ask you to join with me in saluting the members of the Commission who are here tonight and Senate Majority Leader Howard Baker and Speaker Tip O'Neill for a job well done. I hope and pray the bipartisan spirit that guided you in this endeavor will inspire all of us as we face the challenges of the year ahead.

Nearly half a century ago, in this Chamber, another American President, Franklin Delano Roosevelt, in his second State of the Union message, urged America to look to the future, to meet the challenge of change and the need for leadership that looks forward, not backward.

"Throughout the world," he said, "change is the order of the day. In every nation economic problems long in the making have brought crises to (of) many kinds for which the masters of old practice and theory were unprepared." He also reminded us that "the future lies with those wise political leaders who realize that the great public is interested more in Government than in politics."

So, let us, in these next 2 years--men and women of both parties, every political shade--concentrate on the long-range, bipartisan responsibilities of government, not the short-range or short-term temptations of partisan politics.

The problems we inherited were far worse than most inside and out of government had expected; the recession was deeper than most inside and out of government had predicted. Curing those problems has taken more time and a higher toll than any of us wanted. Unemployment is far too high. Projected Federal spending--if government refuses to tighten its own belt-will also be far too high and could weaken and shorten the economic recovery now underway.

This recovery will bring with it a revival of economic confidence and spending for consumer items and capital goods--the stimulus we need to restart our stalled economic engines. The American people have already stepped up their rate of saving, assuring that the funds needed to modernize our factories and improve our technology will once again flow to business and industry.

The inflationary expectations that led to a 21 1/2-percent interest prime rate and soaring mortgage rates 2 years ago are now reduced by almost half. Leaders have started to realize that double-digit inflation is no longer a way of life. I misspoke there. I should have said "lenders."

So, interest rates have tumbled, paving the way for recovery in vital industries like housing and autos.

The early evidence of that recovery has started coming in. Housing starts for the fourth quarter of 1982 were up 45 percent from a year ago, and housing permits, a sure indicator of future growth, were up a whopping 60 percent.

We're witnessing an upsurge of productivity and impressive evidence that American industry will once again become competitive in markets at home and abroad, ensuring more jobs and better incomes for the Nation's work force. But our confidence must also be tempered by realism and patience. Quick fixes and artificial stimulants repeatedly applied over decades are what brought us the inflationary disorders that we've now paid such a heavy price to cure.

The permanent recovery in employment, production, and investment we seek won't come in a sharp, short spurt. It'll build carefully and steadily in the months and years ahead. In the meantime, the challenge of government is to identify the things that we can do now to ease the massive economic transition for the American people.

The Federal budget is both a symptom and a cause of our economic problems. Unless we reduce the dangerous growth rate in government spending, we could face the prospect of sluggish economic growth into the indefinite future. Failure to cope with this problem now could mean as much as a trillion dollars more in national debt in the next 4 years alone. That would average $4,300 in additional debt for every man, woman, child, and baby in our nation.

To assure a sustained recovery, we must continue getting runaway spending under control to bring those deficits down. If we don't, the recovery will be too short, unemployment will remain too high, and we will leave an unconscionable burden of national debt for our children. That we must not do.

Let's be clear about where the deficit problem comes from. Contrary to the drumbeat we've been hearing for the last few months, the deficits we face are not rooted in defense spending. Taken as a percentage of the gross national product, our defense spending happens to be only about four-fifths of what it was in 1970. Nor is the deficit, as some would have it, rooted in tax cuts. Even with our tax cuts, taxes as a fraction of gross national product remain about the same as they were in 1970. The fact is, our deficits come from the uncontrolled growth of the budget for domestic spending.

During the 1970's, the share of our national income devoted to this domestic spending increased by more than 60 percent, from 10 cents out of every dollar produced by the American people to 16 cents. In spite of all our economies and efficiencies, and without adding any new programs, basic, necessary domestic spending provided for in this year's budget will grow to almost a trillion dollars over the next 5 years.

The deficit problem is a clear and present danger to the basic health of our Republic. We need a plan to overcome this danger--a plan based on these principles. It must be bipartisan. Conquering the deficits and putting the Government's house in order will require the best effort of all of us. It must be fair. Just as all will share in the benefits that will come from recovery, all would share fairly in the burden of transition. It must be prudent. The strength of our national defense must be restored so that we can pursue prosperity and peace and freedom while maintaining our commitment to the truly needy. And finally, it must be realistic. We can't rely on hope alone.

With these guiding principles in mind, let me outline a four-part plan to increase economic growth and reduce deficits.

First, in my budget message, I will recommend a Federal spending freeze. I know this is strong medicine, but so far, we have only cut the rate of increase in Federal spending.

The Government has continued to spend more money each year, though not as much more as it did in the past. Taken as a whole, the budget I'm proposing for the fiscal year will increase no more than the rate of inflation. In other words, the Federal Government will hold the line on real spending. Now, that's far less than many American families have had to do in these difficult times.

I will request that the proposed 6-month freeze in cost-of-living adjustments recommended by the bipartisan Social Security Commission be applied to other government-related retirement programs. I will, also, propose a 1-year freeze on a broad range of domestic spending programs, and for Federal civilian and military pay and pension programs. And let me say right here, I'm sorry, with regard to the military, in asking that of them, because for so many years they have been so far behind and so low in reward for what the men and women in uniform are doing. But I'm sure they will understand that this must be across the board and fair.

Second, I will ask the Congress to adopt specific measures to control the growth of the so-called uncontrollable spending programs. These are the automatic spending programs, such as food stamps, that cannot be simply frozen and that have grown by over 400 percent since 1970. They are the largest single cause of the built-in or structural deficit problem. Our standard here will be fairness, ensuring that the taxpayers' hard-earned dollars go only to the truly needy; that none of them are turned away, but that fraud and waste are stamped out. And I'm sorry to say, there's a lot of it out there. In the food stamp program alone, last year, we identified almost $1.1 billion in overpayments. The taxpayers aren't the only victims of this kind of abuse. The truly needy suffer as funds intended for them are taken not by the needy, but by the greedy. For everyone's sake, we must put an end to such waste and corruption.

Third, I will adjust our program to restore America's defenses by proposing $55 billion in defense savings over the next 5 years. These are savings recommended to me by the

Secretary of Defense, who has assured me they can be safely achieved and will not diminish our ability to negotiate arms reductions or endanger America's security. We will not gamble with our national survival.

And fourth, because we must ensure reduction and eventual elimination of deficits over the next several years, I will propose a standby tax, limited to no more than 1 percent of the gross national product, to start in fiscal 1986. It would last no more than 3 years, and it would start only if the Congress has first approved our spending freeze and budget control program. And there are several other conditions also that must be met, all of them in order for this program to be triggered.

Now, you could say that this is an insurance policy for the future, a remedy that will be at hand if needed but only resorted to if absolutely necessary. In the meantime, we'll continue to study ways to simplify the tax code and make it more fair for all Americans. This is a goal that every American who's ever struggled with a tax form can understand.

At the same time, however, I will oppose any efforts to undo the basic tax reforms that we've already enacted, including the 10-percent tax break coming to taxpayers this July and the tax indexing which will protect all Americans from inflationary bracket creep in the years ahead.

Now, I realize that this four-part plan is easier to describe than it will be to enact. But the looming deficits that hang over us and over America's future must be reduced. The path I've outlined is fair, balanced, and realistic. If enacted, it will ensure a steady decline in deficits, aiming toward a balanced budget by the end of the decade. It's the only path that will lead to a strong, sustained recovery. Let us follow that path together.

No domestic challenge is more crucial than providing stable, permanent jobs for all Americans who want to work. The recovery program will provide jobs for most, but others will need special help and training for new skills. Shortly, I will submit to the Congress the Employment Act of 1983,

designed to get at the special problems of the long-term unemployed, as well as young people trying to enter the job
market. I'll propose extending unemployment benefits, including special incentives to employers who hire the long-
term unemployed, providing programs for displaced workers,
and helping federally funded and State-administered unemployment insurance programs provide workers with training
and relocation assistance. Finally, our proposal will include
new incentives for summer youth employment to help young
people get a start in the job market.

We must offer both short-term help and long-term hope
for our unemployed. I hope we can work together on this. I
hope we can work together as we did last year in enacting
the landmark Job Training Partnership Act. Regulatory reform legislation, a responsible clean air act, and passage of
enterprise zone legislation will also create new incentives for
jobs and opportunity.

One of out of every five jobs in our country depends on
trade. So, I will propose a broader strategy in the field of
international trade--one that increases the openness of our
trading system and is fairer to America's farmers and workers in the world marketplace. We must have adequate export
financing to sell American products overseas. I will ask for
new negotiating authority to remove barriers and to get more
of our products into foreign markets. We must strengthen
the organization of our trade agencies and make changes in
our domestic laws and international trade policy to promote
free trade and the increased flow of American goods, services, and investments.

Our trade position can also be improved by making our port
system more efficient. Better, more active harbors translate
into stable jobs in our coalfields, railroads, trucking industry, and ports. After 2 years of debate, it's time for us to get
together and enact a port modernization bill.

Education, training, and retraining are fundamental to our
success as are research and development and productivity.
Labor, management, and government at all levels can and

must participate in improving these tools of growth. Tax policy, regulatory practices, and government programs all need constant reevaluation in terms of our competitiveness. Every American has a role and a stake in international trade.

We Americans are still the technological leaders in most fields. We must keep that edge, and to do so we need to begin renewing the basics--starting with our educational system. While we grew complacent, others have acted. Japan, with a population only about half the size of ours, graduates from its universities more engineers than we do. If a child doesn't receive adequate math and science teaching by the age of 16, he or she has lost the chance to be a scientist or an engineer. We must join together-parents, teachers, grass roots groups, organized labor, and the business community-to revitalize American education by setting a standard of excellence.

In 1983 we seek four major education goals: a quality education initiative to encourage a substantial upgrading of math and science instruction through block grants to the States; establishment of education savings accounts that will give middle and lower-income families an incentive to save for their children's college education and, at the same time, encourage a real increase in savings for economic growth; passage of tuition tax credits for parents who want to send their children to private or religiously affiliated schools; a constitutional amendment to permit voluntary school prayer. God should never have been expelled from America's classrooms in the first place.

Our commitment to fairness means that we must assure legal and economic equity for women, and eliminate, once and for all, all traces of unjust discrimination against women from the United States Code. We will not tolerate wage discrimination based on sex, and we intend to strengthen enforcement of child support laws to ensure that single parents, most of whom are women, do not suffer unfair financial hardship. We will also take action to remedy inequities in pensions. These initiatives will be joined by others to continue our efforts to promote equity for women.

Also in the area of fairness and equity, we will ask for extension of the Civil Rights Commission, which is due to expire this year. The Commission is an important part of the ongoing struggle for justice in America, and we strongly support its reauthorization. Effective enforcement of our nation's fair housing laws is also essential to ensuring equal opportunity. In the year ahead, we'll work to strengthen enforcement of fair housing laws for all Americans.

The time has also come for major reform of our criminal justice statutes and acceleration of the drive against organized crime and drug trafficking. It's high time that we make our cities safe again. This administration hereby declares an all-out war on big-time organized crime and the drug racketeers who are poisoning our young people. We will also implement recommendations of our Task Force on Victims of Crime, which will report to me this week.

American agriculture, the envy of the world, has become the victim of its own successes. With one farmer now producing enough food to feed himself and 77 other people, America is confronted with record surplus crops and commodity prices below the cost of production. We must strive, through innovations like the payment-in-kind crop swap approach and an aggressive export policy, to restore health and vitality to rural America. Meanwhile, I have instructed the Department of Agriculture to work individually with farmers with debt problems to help them through these tough times.

Over the past year, our Task Force on Private Sector Initiatives has successfully forged a working partnership involving leaders of business, labor, education, and government to address the training needs of American workers. Thanks to the Task Force, private sector initiatives are now underway in all 50 States of the Union, and thousands of working people have been helped in making the shift from dead-end jobs and low-demand skills to the growth areas of high technology and the service economy. Additionally, a major effort will be focused on encouraging the expansion of private community child care. The new advisory council on private sector initiatives will carry on and extend this vital work of encouraging private initiative in 1983.

In the coming year, we will also act to improve the quality of life for Americans by curbing the skyrocketing cost of health care that is becoming an unbearable financial burden for so many. And we will submit legislation to provide catastrophic illness insurance coverage for older Americans.

I will also shortly submit a comprehensive federalism proposal that will continue our efforts to restore to States and local governments their roles as dynamic laboratories of change in a creative society.

During the next several weeks, I will send to the Congress a series of detailed proposals on these and other topics and look forward to working with you on the development of these initiatives.

So far, now, I've concentrated mainly on the problems posed by the future. But in almost every home and workplace in America, we're already witnessing reason for great hope--the first flowering of the manmade miracles of high technology, a field pioneered and still led by our country.

To many of us now, computers, silicon chips, data processing, cybernetics, and all the other innovations of the dawning high technology age are as mystifying as the workings of the combustion engine must have been when that first Model T rattled down Main Street, U.S.A. But as surely as America's pioneer spirit made us the industrial giant of the 20th century, the same pioneer spirit today is opening up on another vast front of opportunity, the frontier of high technology.

In conquering the frontier we cannot write off our traditional industries, but we must develop the skills and industries that will make us a pioneer of tomorrow. This administration is committed to keeping America the technological leader of the world now and into the 21st century.

But let us turn briefly to the international arena. America's leadership in the world came to us because of our own strength and because of the values which guide us as a society: free elections, a free press, freedom of religious choice, free trade unions, and above all, freedom for the individual and rejection of the arbitrary power of the state. These values are the bedrock of our strength. They unite us in a stewardship of peace and freedom with our allies and friends in NATO, in Asia, in Latin America, and elsewhere. They are also the values which in the recent past some among us had begun to doubt and view with a cynical eye.

Fortunately, we and our allies have rediscovered the strength of our common democratic values, and we're applying them as a cornerstone of a comprehensive strategy for peace with freedom. In London last year, I announced the commitment of the United States to developing the infrastructure of democracy throughout the world. We intend to pursue this democratic initiative vigorously. The future belongs not to governments and ideologies which oppress their peoples, but to democratic systems of self-government which encourage individual initiative and guarantee personal freedom.

But our strategy for peace with freedom must also be based on strength--economic strength and military strength. A strong American economy is essential to the well-being and security of our friends and allies. The restoration of a strong, healthy American economy has been and remains one of the central pillars of our foreign policy. The progress I've been able to report to you tonight will, I know, be as warmly welcomed by the rest of the world as it is by the American people.

We must also recognize that our own economic well-being is inextricably linked to the world economy. We export over 20 percent of our industrial production, and 40 percent of our farmland produces for export. We will continue to work closely with the industrialized democracies of Europe and Japan and with the International Monetary Fund to ensure it has adequate resources to help bring the world economy back to strong, noninflationary growth.

As the leader of the West and as a country that has become great and rich because of economic freedom, America must be an unrelenting advocate of free trade. As some nations are tempted to turn to protectionism, our strategy cannot be to follow them, but to lead the way toward freer trade. To this end, in May of this year America will host an economic summit meeting in Williamsburg, Virginia.

As we begin our third year, we have put in place a defense program that redeems the neglect of the past decade. We have developed a realistic military strategy to deter threats to peace and to protect freedom if deterrence fails. Our Armed Forces are finally properly paid; after years of neglect are well trained and becoming better equipped and supplied. And the American uniform is once again worn with pride. Most of the major systems needed for modernizing our defenses are already underway, and we will be addressing one key system, the MX missile, in consultation with the Congress in a few months.

America's foreign policy is once again based on bipartisanship, on realism, strength, full partnership, in consultation with our allies, and constructive negotiation with potential adversaries. From the Middle East to southern Africa to Geneva, American diplomats are taking the initiative to make peace and lower arms levels. We should be proud of our role as peacemakers.

In the Middle East last year, the United States played the major role in ending the tragic fighting in Lebanon and negotiated the withdrawal of the PLO from Beirut.

Last September, I outlined principles to carry on the peace process begun so promisingly at Camp David. All the people of the Middle East should know that in the year ahead we will not flag in our efforts to build on that foundation to bring them the blessings of peace.

In Central America and the Caribbean Basin, we are likewise engaged in a partnership for peace, prosperity, and democracy. Final passage of the remaining portions of our Caribbean Basin Initiative, which passed the House last year, is one of this administration's top legislative priorities for 1983.

The security and economic assistance policies of this administration in Latin America and elsewhere are based on realism and represent a critical investment in the future of the human race. This undertaking is a joint responsibility of the executive and legislative branches, and I'm counting on the cooperation and statesmanship of the Congress to help us meet this essential foreign policy goal.

At the heart of our strategy for peace is our relationship with the Soviet Union. The past year saw a change in Soviet leadership. We're prepared for a positive change in Soviet-American relations. But the Soviet Union must show by deeds as well as words a sincere commitment to respect the rights and sovereignty of the family of nations. Responsible members of the world community do not threaten or invade their neighbors. And they restrain their allies from aggression.

For our part, we're vigorously pursuing arms reduction negotiations with the Soviet Union. Supported by our allies, we've put forward draft agreements proposing significant weapon reductions to equal and verifiable lower levels. We insist on an equal balance of forces. And given the overwhelming evidence of Soviet violations of international treaties concerning chemical and biological weapons, we also insist that any agreement we sign can and will be verifiable.

In the case of intermediate-range nuclear forces, we have proposed the complete elimination of the entire class of land-based missiles. We're also prepared to carefully explore serious Soviet proposals. At the same time, let me emphasize that allied steadfastness remains a key to achieving arms reductions.

With firmness and dedication, we'll continue to negotiate. Deep down, the Soviets must know it's in their interest as well as ours to prevent a wasteful arms race. And once they recognize our unshakable resolve to maintain adequate deterrence, they will have every reason to join us in the search for greater security and major arms reductions. When that moment comes--and I'm confident that it will--we will have taken an important step toward a more peaceful future for all the world's people.

A very wise man, Bernard Baruch, once said that America has never forgotten the nobler things that brought her into being and that light her path. Our country is a special place, because we Americans have always been sustained, through good times and bad, by a noble vision--a vision not only of what the world around us is today but what we as a free people can make it be tomorrow.

We're realists; we solve our problems instead of ignoring them, no matter how loud the chorus of despair around us. But we're also idealists, for it was an ideal that brought our ancestors to these shores from every corner of the world.

Right now we need both realism and idealism. Millions of our neighbors are without work. It is up to us to see they aren't without hope. This is a task for all of us. And may I say, Americans have rallied to this cause, proving once again that we are the most generous people on Earth.

We who are in government must take the lead in restoring the economy. And here all that time, I thought you were reading the paper.

The single thing--the single thing that can start the wheels of industry turning again is further reduction of interest rates. Just another 1 or 2 points can mean tens of thousands of jobs.

Right now, with inflation as low as it is, 3.9 percent, there is room for interest rates to come down. Only fear prevents their reduction. A lender, as we know, must charge an interest rate that recovers the depreciated value of the dollars loaned. And that depreciation is, of course, the amount of inflation. Today, interest rates are based on fear--fear that government will resort to measures, as it has in the past, that will send inflation zooming again.

We who serve here in this Capital must erase that fear by making it absolutely clear that we will not stop fighting inflation; that, together, we will do only those things that will lead to lasting economic growth.

Yes, the problems confronting us are large and forbidding. And, certainly, no one can or should minimize the plight of millions of our friends and neighbors who are living in the bleak emptiness of unemployment. But we must and can give them good reason to be hopeful.

Back over the years, citizens like ourselves have gathered within these walls when our nation was threatened; sometimes when its very existence was at stake. Always with courage and common sense, they met the crises of their time and lived to see a stronger, better, and more prosperous country. The present situation is no worse and, in fact, is not as bad as some of those they faced. Time and again, they proved that there is nothing we Americans cannot achieve as free men and women.

Yes, we still have problems--plenty of them. But it's just plain wrong--unjust to our country and unjust to our people--to let those problems stand in the way of the most important truth of all: America is on the mend.

We owe it to the unfortunate to be aware of their plight and to help them in every way we can. No one can quarrel with that. We must and do have compassion for all the victims of this economic crisis. But the big story about America today is the way that millions of confident, caring people-those extraordinary "ordinary" Americans who never make the headlines and will never be interviewed--are laying the foundation, not just for recovery from our present problems but for a better tomorrow for all our people.

From coast to coast, on the job and in classrooms and laboratories, at new construction sites and in churches and community groups, neighbors are helping neighbors. And they've already begun the building, the research, the work, and the giving that will make our country great again.

I believe this, because I believe in them-in the strength of their hearts and minds, in the commitment that each one of them brings to their daily lives, be they high or humble. The challenge for us in government is to be worthy of them--to make government a help, not a hindrance to our people in the challenging but promising days ahead.

If we do that, if we care what our children and our children's children will say of us, if we want them one day to be thankful for what we did here in these temples of freedom, we will work together to make America better for our having been here-not just in this year or this decade but in the next century and beyond.

Thank you, and God bless you.

NOTE: The President spoke at 9:03 p.m. in the House Chamber of the Capitol. He was introduced by Thomas P. O'Neill, Jr., Speaker of the House of Representatives. The address was broadcast live on nationwide radio and television.

State of the Union Address January 25, 1984

Mr. Speaker, Mr. President, distinguished Members of the Congress, honored guests, and fellow citizens:

Once again, in keeping with time-honored tradition, I have come to report to you on the state of the Union, and I'm pleased to report that America is much improved, and there's good reason to believe that improvement will continue through the days to come.

You and I have had some honest and open differences in the year past. But they didn't keep us from joining hands in bipartisan cooperation to stop a long decline that had drained this nation's spirit and eroded its health. There is renewed energy and optimism throughout the land. America is back, standing tall, looking to the eighties with courage, confidence, and hope.

The problems we're overcoming are not the heritage of one person, party, or even one generation. It's just the tendency of government to grow, for practices and programs to become the nearest thing to eternal life we'll ever see on this Earth. And there's always that well-intentioned chorus of voices saying, "With a little more power and a little more money, we could do so much for the people." For a time we forgot the American dream isn't one of making government bigger; it's keeping faith with the mighty spirit of free people under God.

As we came to the decade of the eighties, we faced the worst crisis in our postwar history. In the seventies were years of rising problems and falling confidence. There was a feeling government had grown beyond the consent of the governed. Families felt helpless in the face of mounting inflation and the indignity of taxes that reduced reward for hard work, thrift, and risktaking. All this was overlaid by an evergrowing web of rules and regulations.

On the international scene, we had an uncomfortable feeling that we'd lost the respect of friend and foe. Some questioned whether we had the will to defend peace and freedom. But America is too great for small dreams. There was a hunger in the land for a spiritual revival; if you will, a crusade for renewal. The American people said: Let us look to the future with confidence, both at home and abroad. Let us give freedom a chance.

Americans were ready to make a new beginning, and together we have done it. We're confronting our problems one by one. Hope is alive tonight for millions of young families and senior citizens set free from unfair tax increases and crushing inflation. Inflation has been beaten down from 12.4 to 3.2 percent, and that's a great victory for all the people. The prime rate has been cut almost in half, and we must work together to bring it down even more.

Together, we passed the first across-the-board tax reduction for everyone since the Kennedy tax cuts. Next year, tax rates will be indexed so inflation can't push people into higher brackets when they get cost-of-living pay raises. Government must never again use inflation to profit at the people's expense.

Today a working family earning $25,000 has $1,100 more in purchasing power than if tax and inflation rates were still at the 1980 levels. Real after-tax income increased 5 percent last year. And economic deregulation of key industries like transportation has offered more chances---or choices, I should say, to consumers and new changes---or chances for entrepreneurs and protecting safety. Tonight, we can report and be proud of one of the best recoveries in decades. Send away the handwringers and the doubting Thomases. Hope is reborn for couples dreaming of owning homes and for risktakers with vision to create tomorrow's opportunities.

The spirit of enterprise is sparked by the sunrise industries of high-tech and by small business people with big ideas--

people like Barbara Proctor, who rose from a ghetto to build a multimillion-dollar advertising agency in Chicago; Carlos Perez, a Cuban refugee, who turned $27 and a dream into a successful importing business in Coral Gables, Florida.

People like these are heroes for the eighties. They helped 4 million Americans find jobs in 1983. More people are drawing paychecks tonight than ever before. And Congress helps--or progress helps everyone-well, Congress does too----everyone. In 1983 women filled 73 percent of all the new jobs in managerial, professional, and technical fields.

But we know that many of our fellow countrymen are still out of work, wondering what will come of their hopes and dreams. Can we love America and not reach out to tell them: You are not forgotten; we will not rest until each of you can reach as high as your God-given talents will take you.

The heart of America is strong; it's good and true. The cynics were wrong; America never was a sick society. We're seeing rededication to bedrock values of faith, family, work, neighborhood, peace, and freedom--values that help bring us together as one people, from the youngest child to the most senior citizen.

The Congress deserves America's thanks for helping us restore pride and credibility to our military. And I hope that you're as proud as I am of the young men and women in uniform who have volunteered to man the ramparts in defense of freedom and whose dedication, valor, and skill increases so much our chance of living in a world at peace.

People everywhere hunger for peace and a better life. The tide of the future is a freedom tide, and our struggle for democracy cannot and will not be denied. This nation champions peace that enshrines liberty, democratic rights, and dignity for every individual. America's new strength, confidence, and purpose are carrying hope and opportunity far from our shores. A world economic recovery is underway. It began here.

We've journeyed far, but we have much farther to go.

Franklin Roosevelt told us 50 years ago this month: "Civilization can not go back; civilization must not stand still. We have undertaken new methods. It is our task to perfect, to improve, to alter when necessary, but in all cases to go forward."

It's time to move forward again, time for America to take freedom's next step. Let us unite tonight behind four great goals to keep America free, secure, and at peace in the eighties together.

We can ensure steady economic growth. We can develop America's next frontier. We can strengthen our traditional values. And we can build a meaningful peace to protect our loved ones and this shining star of faith that has guided millions from tyranny to the safe harbor of freedom, progress, and hope.

Doing these things will open wider the gates of opportunity, provide greater security for all, with no barriers of bigotry or discrimination.

The key to a dynamic decade is vigorous economic growth, our first great goal. We might well begin with common sense in Federal budgeting: government spending no more than government takes in.

We must bring Federal deficits down. But how we do that makes all the difference.

We can begin by limiting the size and scope of government. Under the leadership of Vice President Bush, we have reduced the growth of Federal regulations by more than 25 percent and cut well over 300 million hours of government-required paperwork each year. This will save the public more than $150 billion over the next 10 years.

The Grace commission has given us some 2,500 recommendations for reducing wasteful spending, and they're being examined throughout the administration. Federal spending growth has been cut from 17.4 percent in 1980 to less than half of that today, and we have already achieved over $300 billion in budget savings for the period of 1982 to '86.

But that's only a little more than half of what we sought. Government is still spending too large a percentage of the total economy.

Now, some insist that any further budget savings must be obtained by reducing the portion spent on defense. This ignores the fact that national defense is solely the responsibility of the Federal Government; indeed, it is its prime responsibility. And yet defense spending is less than a third of the total budget. During the years of President Kennedy and of the years before that, defense was almost half the total budget. And then came several years in which our military capability was allowed to deteriorate to a very dangerous degree. We are just now restoring, through the essential modernization of our conventional and strategic forces, our capability to meet our present and future security needs. We dare not shirk our responsibility to keep America free, secure, and at peace.

The last decade saw domestic spending surge literally out of control. But the basis for such spending had been laid in previous years. A pattern of overspending has been in place for half a century. As the national debt grew, we were told not to worry, that we owed it to ourselves.

Now we know that deficits are a cause for worry. But there's a difference of opinion as to whether taxes should be increased, spending cut, or some of both. Fear is expressed that government borrowing to fund the deficit could inhibit the economic recovery by taking capital needed for business and industrial expansion. Well, I think that debate is missing an important point. Whether government borrows or increases taxes, it will be taking the same amount of money from the private sector, and, either way, that's too much. Simple fairness dictates that government must not raise taxes on families struggling to pay their bills. The root of the problem is that government's share is more than we can afford if we're to have a sound economy.

We must bring down the deficits to ensure continued economic growth. In the budget that I will submit on February

1st, I will recommend measures that will reduce the deficit over the next 5 years. Many of these will be unfinished business from last year's budget.

Some could be enacted quickly if we could join in a serious effort to address this problem. I spoke today with Speaker of the House O'Neill, Senate Majority Leader Baker, Senate Minority Leader Byrd, and House Minority Leader Michel. I asked them if they would designate congressional representatives to meet with representatives of the administration to try to reach prompt agreement on a bipartisan deficit reduction plan. I know it would take a long, hard struggle to agree on a full-scale plan. So, what I have proposed is that we first see if we can agree on a down payment.

Now, I believe there is basis for such an agreement, one that could reduce the deficits by about a hundred billion dollars over the next 3 years. We could focus on some of the less contentious spending cuts that are still pending before the Congress. These could be combined with measures to close certain tax loopholes, measures that the Treasury Department has previously said to be worthy of support. In addition, we could examine the possibility of achieving further outlay savings based on the work of the Grace commission.

If the congressional leadership is willing, my representatives will be prepared to meet with theirs at the earliest possible time. I would hope the leadership might agree on an expedited timetable in which to develop and enact that down payment.

But a down payment alone is not enough to break us out of the deficit problem. It could help us start on the right path. Yet, we must do more. So, I propose that we begin exploring how together we can make structural reforms to curb the built-in growth of spending.

I also propose improvements in the budgeting process. Some 43 of our 50 States grant their Governors the right to veto individual items in appropriation bills without having to veto the entire bill. California is one of those 43 States. As Governor, I found this line-item veto was a powerful tool against wasteful or extravagant spending. It works in 43 States. Let's put it to work in Washington for all the people.

It would be most effective if done by constitutional amendment. The majority of Americans approve of such an amendment, just as they and I approve of an amendment mandating a balanced Federal budget. Many States also have this protection in their constitutions.

To talk of meeting the present situation by increasing taxes is a Band-Aid solution which does nothing to cure an illness that's been coming on for half a century--to say nothing of the fact that it poses a real threat to economic recovery. Let's remember that a substantial amount of income tax is presently owed and not paid by people in the underground economy. It would be immoral to make those who are paying taxes pay more to compensate for those who aren't paying their share.

There's a better way. Let us go forward with an historic reform for fairness, simplicity, and incentives for growth. I am asking Secretary Don Regan for a plan for action to simplify the entire tax code, so all taxpayers, big and small, are treated more fairly. And I believe such a plan could result in that underground economy being brought into the sunlight of honest tax compliance. And it could make the tax base broader, so personal tax rates could come down, not go up. I've asked that specific recommendations, consistent with those objectives, be presented to me by December 1984.

Our second great goal is to build on America's pioneer spirit--I said something funny? I said America's next frontier--and that's to develop that frontier. A sparkling economy spurs initiatives, sunrise industries, and makes older ones more competitive.

Nowhere is this more important than our next frontier: space. Nowhere do we so effectively demonstrate our technological leadership and ability to make life better on Earth. The Space Age is barely a quarter of a century old. But already we've pushed civilization forward with our advances in science and technology. Opportunities and jobs will multiply as we cross new thresholds of knowledge and reach deeper into the unknown.

Our progress in space--taking giant steps for all mankind--is a tribute to American teamwork and excellence. Our finest minds in government, industry, and academia have all pulled together. And we can be proud to say: We are first; we are the best; and we are so because we're free.

America has always been greatest when we dared to be great. We can reach for greatness again. We can follow our dreams to distant stars, living and working in space for peaceful, economic, and scientific gain. Tonight, I am directing NASA to develop a permanently manned space station and to do it within a decade.

A space station will permit quantum leaps in our research in science, communications, in metals, and in lifesaving medicines which could be manufactured only in space. We want our friends to help us meet these challenges and share in their benefits. NASA will invite other countries to participate so we can strengthen peace, build prosperity, and expand freedom for all who share our goals.

Just as the oceans opened up a new world for clipper ships and Yankee traders, space holds enormous potential for commerce today. The market for space transportation could surpass our capacity to develop it. Companies interested in putting payloads into space must have ready access to private sector launch services. The Department of Transportation will help an expendable launch services industry to get off the ground. We'll soon implement a number of executive initiatives, develop proposals to ease regulatory constraints, and, with NASA's help, promote private sector investment in space.

And as we develop the frontier of space, let us remember our responsibility to preserve our older resources here on Earth. Preservation of our environment is not a liberal or conservative challenge, it's common sense.

Though this is a time of budget constraints, I have requested for EPA one of the largest percentage budget increases of any agency. We will begin the long, necessary effort to clean up a productive recreational area and a special national resource--the Chesapeake Bay.

To reduce the threat posed by abandoned hazardous waste dumps, EPA will spend $410 million. And I will request a supplemental increase of 50 million. And because the Superfund law expires in 1985, I've asked Bill Ruckelshaus to develop a proposal for its extension so there'll be additional time to complete this important task.

On the question of acid rain, which concerns people in many areas of the United States and Canada, I'm proposing a research program that doubles our current funding. And we'll take additional action to restore our lakes and develop new technology to reduce pollution that causes acid rain.

We have greatly improved the conditions of our natural resources. We'll ask the Congress for $157 million beginning in 1985 to acquire new park and conservation lands. The Department of the Interior will encourage careful, selective exploration and production on our vital resources in an Exclusive Economic Zone within the 200-mile limit off our coasts--but with strict adherence to environmental laws and with fuller State and public participation.

But our most precious resources, our greatest hope for the future, are the minds and hearts of our people, especially our children. We can help them build tomorrow by strengthening our community of shared values. This must be our third great goal. For us, faith, work, family, neighborhood, freedom, and peace are not just words; they're expressions of what America means, definitions of what makes us a good and loving people.

Families stand at the center of our society. And every family has a personal stake in promoting excellence in education. Excellence does not begin in Washington. A 600-percent increase in Federal spending on education between 1960 and 1980 was accompanied by a steady decline in Scholastic Aptitude Test scores. Excellence must begin in our homes and neighborhood schools, where it's the responsibility of every parent and teacher and the right of every child.

Our children come first, and that's why I established a bi-partisan National Commission on Excellence in Education, to help us chart a commonsense course for better education. And already, communities are implementing the Commission's recommendations. Schools are reporting progress in math and reading skills. But we must do more to restore discipline to schools; and we must encourage the teaching of new basics, reward teachers of merit, enforce tougher standards, and put our parents back in charge.

I will continue to press for tuition tax credits to expand opportunities for families and to soften the double payment for those paying public school taxes and private school tuition. Our proposal would target assistance to low- and middle-income families. Just as more incentives are needed within our schools, greater competition is needed among our schools. Without standards and competition, there can be no champions, no records broken, no excellence in education or any other walk of life.

And while I'm on this subject, each day your Members observe a 200-year-old tradition meant to signify America is one nation under God. I must ask: If you can begin your day with a member of the clergy standing right here leading you in prayer, then why can't freedom to acknowledge God be enjoyed again by children in every schoolroom across this land?

America was founded by people who believed that God was their rock of safety. He is ours. I recognize we must be cautious in claiming that God is on our side, but I think it's all right to keep asking if we're on His side.

During our first 3 years, we have joined bipartisan efforts to restore protection of the law to unborn children. Now, I know this issue is very controversial. But unless and until it can be proven that an unborn child is not a living human being, can we justify assuming without proof that it isn't? No one has yet offered such proof; indeed, all the evidence is to the contrary. We should rise above bitterness and reproach, and if Americans could come together in a spirit of understanding and helping, then we could find positive solutions to the tragedy of abortion.

Economic recovery, better education, rededication to values, all show the spirit of renewal gaining the upper hand. And all will improve family life in the eighties. But families need more. They need assurance that they and their loved ones can walk the streets of America without being afraid. Parents need to know their children will not be victims of child pornography and abduction. This year we will intensify our drive against these and other horrible crimes like sexual abuse and family violence.

Already our efforts to crack down on career criminals, organized crime, drugpushers, and to enforce tougher sentences and paroles are having effect. In 1982 the crime rate dropped by 4.3 percent, the biggest decline since 1972. Protecting victims is just as important as safeguarding the rights of defendants.

Opportunities for all Americans will increase if we move forward in fair housing and work to ensure women's rights, provide for equitable treatment in pension benefits and Individual Retirement Accounts, facilitate child care, and enforce delinquent parent support payments.

It's not just the home but the workplace and community that sustain our values and shape our future. So, I ask your help in assisting more communities to break the bondage of dependency. Help us to free enterprise by permitting debate and voting "yes" on our proposal for enterprise zones in America. This has been before you for 2 years. Its passage can help high-unemployment areas by creating jobs and restoring neighborhoods.

A society bursting with opportunities, reaching for its future with confidence, sustained by faith, fair play, and a conviction that good and courageous people will flourish when they're free--these are the secrets of a strong and prosperous America at peace with itself and the world.

A lasting and meaningful peace is our fourth great goal. It is our highest aspiration. And our record is clear: Americans resort to force only when we must. We have never been aggressors. We have always struggled to defend freedom and democracy.

We have no territorial ambitions. We occupy no countries. We build no walls to lock people in. Americans build the future. And our vision of a better life for farmers, merchants, and working people, from the Americas to Asia, begins with a simple premise: The future is best decided by ballots, not bullets.

Governments which rest upon the consent of the governed do not wage war on their neighbors. Only when people are given a personal stake in deciding their own destiny, benefiting from their own risks, do they create societies that are prosperous, progressive, and free. Tonight, it is democracies that offer hope by feeding the hungry, prolonging life, and eliminating drudgery.

When it comes to keeping America strong, free, and at peace, there should be no Republicans or Democrats, just patriotic Americans. We can decide the tough issues not by who is right, but by what is right.

Together, we can continue to advance our agenda for peace. We can establish a more stable basis for peaceful relations with the Soviet Union; strengthen allied relations across the board; achieve real and equitable reductions in the levels of nuclear arms; reinforce our peacemaking efforts in the Middle East, Central America, and southern Africa; or assist developing countries, particularly our neighbors in the Western Hemisphere; and assist in the development of democratic institutions throughout the world.

The wisdom of our bipartisan cooperation was seen in the work of the Scowcroft commission, which strengthened our ability to deter war and protect peace. In that same spirit, I urge you to move forward with the Henry Jackson plan to implement the recommendations of the Bipartisan Commission on Central America.

Your joint resolution on the multinational peacekeeping force in Lebanon is also serving the cause of peace. We are making progress in Lebanon. For nearly 10 years, the Lebanese have lived from tragedy to tragedy with no hope for their future. Now the multinational peacekeeping force and our marines are helping them break their cycle of despair. There is hope for a free, independent, and sovereign Lebanon. We must have the courage to give peace a chance. And we must not be driven from our objectives for peace in Lebanon by state-sponsored terrorism. We have seen this ugly specter in Beirut, Kuwait, and Rangoon. It demands international attention. I will forward shortly legislative proposals to help combat terrorism. And I will be seeking support from our allies for concerted action.

Our NATO alliance is strong. 1983 was a banner year for political courage. And we have strengthened our partnerships and our friendships in the Far East. We're committed to dialog, deterrence, and promoting prosperity. We'll work with our trading partners for a new round of negotiations in support of freer world trade, greater competition, and more open markets.

A rebirth of bipartisan cooperation, of economic growth, and military deterrence, and a growing spirit of unity among our people at home and our allies abroad underline a fundamental and far-reaching change: The United States is safer, stronger, and more secure in 1984 than before. We can now move with confidence to seize the opportunities for peace, and we will.

Tonight, I want to speak to the people of the Soviet Union, to tell them it's true that our governments have had serious differences, but our sons and daughters have never fought each other in war. And if we Americans have our way, they never will.

People of the Soviet Union, there is only one sane policy, for your country and mine, to preserve our civilization in this modern age: A nuclear war cannot be won and must never be fought. The only value in our two nations possessing nuclear weapons is to make sure they will never be used. But then would it not be better to do away with them entirely?

People of the Soviet, President Dwight Eisenhower, who fought by your side in World War II, said the essential struggle "is not merely man against man or nation against nation. It is man against war." Americans are people of peace. If your government wants peace, there will be peace. We can come together in faith and friendship to build a safer and far better world for our children and our children's children. And the whole world will rejoice. That is my message to you.

Some days when life seems hard and we reach out for values to sustain us or a friend to help us, we find a person who reminds us what it means to be Americans.

Sergeant Stephen Trujillo, a medic in the 2d Ranger Battalion, 75th Infantry, was in the first helicopter to land at the compound held by Cuban forces in Grenada. He saw three other helicopters crash. Despite the imminent explosion of the burning aircraft, he never hesitated. He ran across 25 yards of open terrain through enemy fire to rescue wounded soldiers. He directed two other medics, administered first aid, and returned again and again to the crash site to carry his wounded friends to safety.

Sergeant Trujillo, you and your fellow service men and women not only saved innocent lives; you set a nation free. You inspire us as a force for freedom, not for despotism; and, yes, for peace, not conquest. God bless you.

And then there are unsung heroes: single parents, couples, church and civic volunteers. Their hearts carry without complaint the pains of family and community problems. They soothe our sorrow, heal our wounds, calm our fears, and share our joy.

A person like Father Ritter is always there. His Covenant House programs in New York and Houston provide shelter and help to thousands of frightened and abused children each year. The same is true of Dr. Charles Carson. Paralyzed in a plane crash, he still believed nothing is impossible. Today in Minnesota, he works 80 hours a week without pay, helping pioneer the field of computer-controlled walking. He has given hope to 500,000 paralyzed Americans that some day they may walk again.

How can we not believe in the greatness of America? How can we not do what is right and needed to preserve this last best hope of man on Earth? After all our struggles to restore America, to revive confidence in our country, hope for our future, after all our hard-won victories earned through the patience and courage of every citizen, we cannot, must not, and will not turn back. We will finish our job. How could we do less? We're Americans.

Carl Sandburg said, "I see America not in the setting sun of a black night of despair • . . I see America in the crimson light of a rising sun fresh from the burning, creative hand of God... I see great days ahead for men and women of will and vision."

I've never felt more strongly that America's best days and democracy's best days lie ahead. We're a powerful force for good. With faith and courage, we can perform great deeds and take freedom's next step. And we will. We will carry on the tradition of a good and worthy people who have brought light where there was darkness, warmth where there was cold, medicine where there was disease, food where there was hunger, and peace where there was only bloodshed.

Let us be sure that those who come after will say of us in our time, that in our time we did everything that could be done. We finished the race; we kept them free; we kept the faith.

Thank you very much. God bless you, and God bless America.

NOTE: The President spoke at 9:02 p.m. in the House Chamber of the Capitol He was introduced by Thomas P. O'Neill, Jr., Speaker of the House of Representatives. The address was broadcast live on nationwide radio and television.

State of the Union Address February 6, 1985

Mr. Speaker, Mr. President, distinguished Members of the Congress, honored guests, and fellow citizens:

I come before you to report on the state of our Union, and I'm pleased to report that after 4 years of united effort, the American people have brought forth a nation renewed, stronger, freer, and more secure than before.

Four years ago we began to change, forever I hope, our assumptions about government and its place in our lives. Out of that change has come great and robust growth-in our confidence, our economy, and our role in the world.

Tonight America is stronger because of the values that we hold dear. We believe faith and freedom must be our guiding stars, for they show us truth, they make us brave, give us hope, and leave us wiser than we were. Our progress began not in Washington, DC, but in the hearts of our families, communities, workplaces, and voluntary groups which, together, are unleashing the invincible spirit of one great nation under God.

Four years ago we said we would invigorate our economy by giving people greater freedom and incentives to take risks and letting them keep more of what they earned. We did what we promised, and a great industrial giant is reborn.

Tonight we can take pride in 25 straight months of economic growth, the strongest in 34 years; a 3-year inflation average of 3.9 percent, the lowest in 17 years; and 7.3 million new jobs in 2 years, with more of our citizens working than ever before.

New freedom in our lives has planted the rich seeds for future success:

For an America of wisdom that honors the family, knowing that if (as) the family goes, so goes our civilization;

For an America of vision that sees tomorrow's dreams in the learning and hard work we do today;

For an America of courage whose service men and women, even as we meet, proudly stand watch on the frontiers of freedom;

For an America of compassion that opens its heart to those who cry out for help.

We have begun well. But it's only a beginning. We're not here to congratulate ourselves on what we have done but to challenge ourselves to finish what has not yet been done.

We're here to speak for millions in our inner cities who long for real jobs, safe neighborhoods, and schools that truly teach. We're here to speak for the American farmer, the entrepreneur, and every worker in industries fighting to modernize and compete. And, yes, we're here to stand, and proudly so, for all who struggle to break free from totalitarianism, for all who know in their hearts that freedom is the one true path to peace and human happiness.

Proverbs tell us, without a vision the people perish. When asked what great principle holds our Union together, Abraham Lincoln said: "Something in (the) Declaration giving liberty, not alone to the people of this country, but hope to the world for all future time."

We honor the giants of our history not by going back but forward to the dreams their vision foresaw. My fellow citizens, this nation is poised for greatness. The time has come to proceed toward a great new challenge--a second American Revolution of hope and opportunity; a revolution carrying us to new heights of progress by pushing back frontiers of knowledge and space; a revolution of spirit that taps the soul of America, enabling us to summon greater strength than we've ever known; and a revolution that carries beyond our shores the golden promise of human freedom in a world of peace.

Let us begin by challenging our conventional wisdom. There are no constraints on the human mind, no walls around the human spirit, no barriers to our progress except those we ourselves erect. Already, pushing down tax rates has freed our economy to vault forward to record growth.

In Europe, they're calling it "the American Miracle." Day by day, we're shattering accepted notions of what is possible. When I was growing up, we failed to see how a new thing called radio would transform our marketplace. Well, today, many have not yet seen how advances in technology are transforming our lives.

In the late 1950's workers at the AT&T semiconductor plant in Pennsylvania produced five transistors a day for $7.50 apiece. They now produce over a million for less than a penny apiece.

New laser techniques could revolutionize heart bypass surgery, cut diagnosis time for viruses linked to cancer from weeks to minutes, reduce hospital costs dramatically, and hold out new promise for saving human lives.

Our automobile industry has overhauled assembly lines, increased worker productivity, and is competitive once again.

We stand on the threshold of a great ability to produce more, do more, be more. Our economy is not getting older and weaker; it's getting younger and stronger. It doesn't need rest and supervision; it needs new challenge, greater freedom. And that word "freedom" is the key to the second American revolution that we need to bring about.

Let us move together with an historic reform of tax simplification for fairness and growth. Last year I asked Treasury Secretary-then-Regan to develop a plan to simplify the tax code, so all taxpayers would be treated more fairly and personal tax rates could come further down.

We have cut tax rates by almost 25 percent, yet the tax system remains unfair and limits our potential for growth. Exclusions and exemptions cause similar incomes to be taxed at different levels. Low-income families face steep tax barriers that make hard lives even harder. The Treasury Department has produced an excellent reform plan, whose principles will guide the final proposal that we will ask you to enact.

One thing that tax reform will not be is a tax increase in disguise. We will not jeopardize the mortgage interest deduction that families need. We will reduce personal tax rates as low as possible by removing many tax preferences. We will propose a top rate of no more than 35 percent, and possibly lower. And we will propose reducing corporate rates, while maintaining incentives for capital formation.

To encourage opportunity and jobs rather than dependency and welfare, we will propose that individuals living at or near the poverty line be totally exempt from Federal income tax. To restore fairness to families, we will propose increasing significantly the personal exemption.

And tonight, I am instructing Treasury Secretary James Baker--I have to get used to saying that--to begin working with congressional authors and committees for bipartisan legislation conforming to these principles. We will call upon the American people for support and upon every man and woman in this Chamber. Together, we can pass, this year, a tax bill for fairness, simplicity, and growth, making this economy the engine of our dreams and America the investment capital of the world. So let us begin.

Tax simplification will be a giant step toward unleashing the tremendous pent-up power of our economy. But a second American revolution must carry the promise of opportunity for all. It is time to liberate the spirit of enterprise in the most distressed areas of our country.

This government will meet its responsibility to help those in need. But policies that increase dependency, break up families, and destroy self-respect are not progressive; they're reactionary. Despite our strides in civil rights, blacks, Hispanics, and all minorities will not have full and equal power until they have full economic power.

We have repeatedly sought passage of enterprise zones to help those in the abandoned corners of our land find jobs, learn skills, and build better lives. This legislation is supported by a majority of you.

Mr. Speaker, I know we agree that 'there must be no forgotten Americans. Let us place new dreams in a million hearts and create a new generation of entrepreneurs by passing enterprise zones this year. And, Tip, you could make that a birthday present.

Nor must we lose the chance to pass our youth employment opportunity wage proposal. We can help teenagers, who have the highest unemployment rate, find summer jobs, so they can know the pride of work and have confidence in their futures.

We'll continue to support the Job Training Partnership Act, which has a nearly two-thirds job placement rate. Credits in education and health care vouchers will help working families shop for services that they need.

Our administration is already encouraging certain low-income public housing residents to own and manage their own dwellings. It's time that all public housing residents have that opportunity of ownership.

The Federal Government can help create a new atmosphere of freedom. But States and localities, many of which enjoy surpluses from the recovery, must not permit their tax and regulatory policies to stand as barriers to growth.

Let us resolve that we will stop spreading dependency and start spreading opportunity; that we will stop spreading bondage and start spreading freedom.

There are some who say that growth initiatives must await final action on deficit reductions. Well, the best way to reduce deficits is through economic growth. More businesses will be started, more investments made, more jobs created, and more people will be on payrolls paying taxes. The best way to reduce government spending is to reduce the need for spending by increasing prosperity. Each added percentage

point per year of real GNP growth will lead to cumulative reduction in deficits of nearly $200 billion over 5 years.

To move steadily toward a balanced budget, we must also
lighten government's claim on our total economy. We will
not do this by raising taxes. We must make sure that our
economy grows faster than the growth in spending by the
Federal Government. In our fiscal year 1986 budget, overall
government program spending will be frozen at the current
level. It must not be one dime higher than fiscal year 1985,
and three points are key.

First, the social safety net for the elderly, the needy, the
disabled, and unemployed will be left intact. Growth of our
major health care programs, Medicare and Medicaid, will be
slowed, but protections for the elderly and needy will be preserved.

Second, we must not relax our efforts to restore military
strength just as we near our goal of a fully equipped, trained,
and ready professional corps. National security is government's first responsibility; so in past years defense spending
took about half the Federal budget. Today it takes less than
a third. We've already reduced our planned defense expenditures by nearly a hundred billion dollars over the past 4
years and reduced projected spending again this year.

You know, we only have a military-industrial complex until a time of danger, and then it becomes the arsenal of democracy. Spending for defense is investing in things that are
priceless--peace and freedom.

Third, we must reduce or eliminate costly government subsidies. For example, deregulation of the airline industry has
led to cheaper airfares, but on Amtrak taxpayers pay about
$35 per passenger every time an Amtrak train leaves the sta-
tion, It's time we ended this huge Federal subsidy.

Our farm program costs have quadrupled in recent years.
Yet I know from visiting farmers, many in great financial dis-
tress, that we need an orderly transition to a market-orient-
ed farm economy. We can help farmers best not by expand-

ing Federal payments but by making fundamental reforms, keeping interest rates heading down, and knocking down foreign trade barriers to American farm exports.

We're moving ahead with Grace commission reforms to eliminate waste and improve government's management practices. In the long run, we must protect the taxpayers from government. And I ask again that you pass, as 32 States have now called for, an amendment mandating the Federal Government spend no more than it takes in. And I ask for the authority, used responsibly by 43 Governors, to veto individual items in appropriation bills. Senator Mattingly has introduced a bill permitting a 2-year trial run of the line-item veto. I hope you'll pass and send that legislation to my desk.

Nearly 50 years of government living beyond its means has brought us to a time of reckoning. Ours is but a moment in history. But one moment of courage, idealism, and bipartisan unity can change American history forever.

Sound monetary policy is key to long-running economic strength and stability. We will continue to cooperate with the Federal Reserve Board, seeking a steady policy that ensures price stability without keeping interest rates artificially high or needlessly holding down growth.

Reducing unneeded red tape and regulations, and deregulating the energy, transportation, and financial industries have unleashed new competition, giving consumers more choices, better services, and lower prices. In just one set of grant programs we have reduced 905 pages of regulations to 31. We seek to fully deregulate natural gas to bring on new supplies and bring us closer to energy independence. Consistent with safety standards, we will continue removing restraints on the bus and railroad industries, we will soon end up legislation---or send up legislation, I should say--to return Conrail to the private sector where it belongs, and we will support further deregulation of the trucking industry.

Every dollar the Federal Government does not take from us, every decision it does not make for us will make our economy stronger, our lives more abundant, our future more free.

Our second American revolution will push on to new possibilities not only on Earth but in the next frontier of space. Despite budget restraints, we will seek record funding for research and development.

We've seen the success of the space shuttle. Now we're going to develop a permanently manned space station and new opportunities for free enterprise, because in the next decade Americans and our friends around the world will be living and working together in space.

In the zero gravity of space, we could manufacture in 30 days lifesaving medicines it would take 30 years to make on Earth. We can make crystals of exceptional purity to produce super computers, creating jobs, technologies, and medical breakthroughs beyond anything we ever dreamed possible.

As we do all this, we'll continue to protect our natural resources. We will seek reauthorization and expanded funding for the Superfund program to continue cleaning up hazardous waste sites which threaten human health and the environment.

Now, there's another great heritage to speak of this evening. Of all the changes that have swept America the past 4 years, none brings greater promise than our rediscovery of the values of faith, freedom, family, work, and neighborhood.

We see signs of renewal in increased attendance in places of worship; renewed optimism and faith in our future; love of country rediscovered by our young, who are leading the way. We've rediscovered that work is good in and of itself, that it ennobles us to create and contribute no matter how seemingly humble our jobs. We've seen a powerful new current from an old and honorable tradition--American generosity.

From thousands answering Peace Corps appeals to help boost food production in Africa, to millions volunteering time, corporations adopting schools, and communities pulling together to help the neediest among us at home, we have refound our values. Private sector initiatives are crucial to our future.

I thank the Congress for passing equal access legislation giving religious groups the same right to use classrooms after school that other groups enjoy. But no citizen need tremble, nor the world shudder, if a child stands in a classroom and breathes a prayer. We ask you again, give children back a right they had for a century and a half or more in this country.

The question of abortion grips our nation. Abortion is either the taking of a human life or it isn't. And if it is--and medical technology is increasingly showing it is--it must be stopped. It is a terrible irony that while some turn to abortion, so many others who cannot become parents cry out for children to adopt. We have room for these children. We can fill the cradles of those who want a child to love. And tonight I ask you in the Congress to move this year on legislation to protect the unborn.

In the area of education, we're returning to excellence, and again, the heroes are our people, not government. We're stressing basics of discipline, rigorous testing, and homework, while helping children become computer-smart as well. For 20 years scholastic aptitude test scores of our high school students went down, but now they have gone up 2 of the last 3 years. We must go forward in our commitment to the new basics, giving parents greater authority and making sure good teachers are rewarded for hard work and achievement through merit pay.

Of all the changes in the past 20 years, none has more threatened our sense of national well-being than the explosion of violent crime. One does not have to be attacked to be a victim. The woman who must run to her car after shopping at night is a victim. The couple draping their door with locks and chains are victims; as is the tired, decent cleaning woman who can't ride a subway home without being afraid.

We do not seek to violate the rights of defendants. But shouldn't we feel more compassion for the victims of crime than for those who commit crime? For the first time in 20 years, the crime index has fallen 2 years in a row. We've convicted over 7,400 drug offenders and put them, as well as leaders of organized crime, behind bars in record numbers.

But we must do more. I urge the House to follow the Senate and enact proposals permitting use of all reliable evidence that police officers acquire in good faith. These proposals would also reform the habeas corpus laws and allow, in keeping with the will of the overwhelming majority of Americans, the use of the death penalty where necessary.

There can be no economic revival in ghettos when the most violent among us are allowed to roam free. It's time we restored domestic tranquility. And we mean to do just that.

Just as we're positioned as never before to secure justice in our economy, we're poised as never before to create a safer, freer, more peaceful world. Our alliances are stronger than ever. Our economy is stronger than ever. We have resumed our historic role as a leader of the free world. And all of these together are a great force for peace.

Since 1981 we've been committed to seeking fair and verifiable arms agreements that would lower the risk of war and reduce the size of nuclear arsenals. Now our determination to maintain a strong defense has influenced the Soviet Union to return to the bargaining table. Our negotiators must be able to go to that table with the united support of the American people. All of us have no greater dream than to see the day when nuclear weapons are banned from this Earth forever.

Each Member of the Congress has a role to play in modernizing our defenses, thus supporting our chances for a meaningful arms agreement. Your vote this spring on the Peacekeeper missile will be a critical test of our resolve to maintain the strength we need and move toward mutual and verifiable arms reductions.

For the past 20 years we've believed that no war will be launched as long as each side knows it can retaliate with a deadly counterstrike. Well, I believe there's a better way of eliminating the threat of nuclear war. It is a Strategic Defense Initiative aimed ultimately at finding a nonnuclear defense against ballistic missiles. It's the most hopeful possibility of the nuclear age. But it's not very well understood.

Some say it will bring war to the heavens, but its purpose is to deter war in the heavens and on Earth. Now, some say the research would be expensive. Perhaps, but it could save millions of lives, indeed humanity itself. And some say if we build such a system, the Soviets will build a defense system of their own. Well, they already have strategic defenses that surpass ours; a civil defense system, where we have almost none; and a research program covering roughly the same areas of technology that we're now exploring. And finally some say the research will take a long time. Well, the answer to that is: Let's get started.

Harry Truman once said that, ultimately, our security and the world's hopes for peace and human progress "lie not in measures of defense or in the control of weapons, but in the growth and expansion of freedom and self-government."

And tonight, we declare anew to our fellow citizens of the world: Freedom is not the sole prerogative of a chosen few; it is the universal right of all God's children. Look to where peace and prosperity flourish today. It is in homes that freedom built. Victories against poverty are greatest and peace most secure where people live by laws that ensure free press, free speech, and freedom to worship, vote, and create wealth.

Our mission is to nourish and defend freedom and democracy, and to communicate these ideals everywhere we can. America's economic success is freedom's success; it can be repeated a hundred times in a hundred different nations. Many countries in east Asia and the Pacific have few resources other than the enterprise of their own people. But through low tax rates and free markets they've soared ahead of centralized economies. And now China is opening up its economy to meet its needs.

We need a stronger and simpler approach to the process of making and implementing trade policy, and we'll be studying potential changes in that process in the next few weeks. We've seen the benefits of free trade and lived through the

disasters of protectionism. Tonight I ask all our trading partners, developed and developing alike, to join us in a new
round of trade negotiations to expand trade and competition
and strengthen the global economy--and to begin it in this
next year.

There are more than 3 billion human beings living in Third
World countries with an average per capita income of $650
a year. Many are victims of dictatorships that impoverished
them with taxation and corruption. Let us ask our allies to
join us in a practical program of trade and assistance that
fosters economic development through personal incentives
to help these people climb from poverty on their own.

We cannot play innocents abroad in a world that's not innocent; nor can we be passive when freedom is under siege.
Without resources, diplomacy cannot succeed. Our security assistance programs help friendly governments defend
themselves and give them confidence to work for peace. And
I hope that you in the Congress will understand that, dollar
for dollar, security assistance contributes as much to global
security as our own defense budget.

We must stand by all our democratic allies. And we must
not break faith with those who are risking their lives---on every continent, from Afghanistan to Nicaragua--to defy Sovi-
et-supported aggression and secure rights which have been
ours from birth.

The Sandinista dictatorship of Nicaragua, with full Cu-
ban-Soviet bloc support, not only persecutes its people, the
church, and denies a free press, but arms and provides bas-
es for Communist terrorists attacking neighboring states.
Support for freedom fighters is self-defense and totally consistent with the OAS and U.N. Charters. It is essential that
the Congress continue all facets of our assistance to Central
America. I want to work with you to support the democratic
forces whose struggle is tied to our own security.

And tonight, I've spoken of great plans and great dreams.
They're dreams we can make come true. Two hundred years
of American history should have taught us that nothing is

impossible.

Ten years ago a young girl left Vietnam with her family, part of the exodus that followed the fall of Saigon. They came to the United States with no possessions and not knowing a word of English. Ten years ago--the young girl studied hard, learned English, and finished high school in the top of her class. And this May, May 22d to be exact, is a big date on her calendar. Just 10 years from the time she left Vietnam, she will graduate from the United States Military Academy at West Point. I thought you might like to meet an American hero named Jean Nguyen.

Now, there's someone else here tonight, born 79 years ago. She lives in the inner city, where she cares for infants born of mothers who are heroin addicts. The children, born in withdrawal, are sometimes even dropped on her doorstep. She helps them with love. Go to her house some night, and maybe you'll see her silhouette against the window as she walks the floor talking softly, soothing a child in her arms-Mother Hale of Harlem, and she, too, is an American hero.

Jean, Mother Hale, your lives tell us that the oldest American saying is new again: Anything is possible in America if we have the faith, the will, and the heart. History is asking us once again to be a force for good in the world. Let us begin in unity, with justice, and love.

Thank you, and God bless you.

NOTE: The President spoke at 9:05 p.m. in the House Chamber of the Capitol. He was introduced by Thomas P. O'Neill, Jr., Speaker of the House of Representatives. The address was broadcast live on nationwide radio and television.

State of the Union Address
February 4, 1986

Mr. Speaker, Mr. President, distinguished Members of the Congress, honored guests, and fellow citizens:

Thank you for allowing me to delay my address until this evening. We paused together to mourn and honor the valor of our seven Challenger heroes. And I hope that we are now ready to do what they would want us to do: Go forward, America, and reach for the stars. We will never forget those brave seven, but we shall go forward.

Mr. Speaker, before I begin my prepared remarks, may I point out that tonight marks the 10th and last State of the Union Message that you've presided over. And on behalf of the American people, I want to salute you for your service to Congress and country. Here's to you!

I have come to review with you the progress of our nation, to speak of unfinished work, and to set our sights on the future. I am pleased to report the state of our Union is stronger than a year ago and growing stronger each day. Tonight we look out on a rising America, firm of heart, united in spirit, powerful in pride and patriotism. America is on the move! But it wasn't long ago that we looked out on a different land: locked factory gates, long gasoline lines, intolerable prices, and interest rates turning the greatest country on Earth into a land of broken dreams. Government growing beyond our consent had become a lumbering giant, slamming shut the gates of opportunity, threatening to crush the very roots of our freedom. What brought America back? The American people brought us back with quiet courage and common sense, with undying faith that in this nation under God the future will be ours; for the future belongs to the free.

Tonight the American people deserve our thanks for 37 straight months of economic growth, for sunrise firms and modernized industries creating 9 million new jobs in 3 years, interest rates cut in half, inflation falling over from 12 percent in 1980 to under 4 today, and a mighty river of good works- a record $74 billion in voluntary giving just last year alone. And despite the pressures of our modern world, family and community remain the moral core of our society, guardians of our values and hopes for the future. Family and community are the costars of this great American comeback. They are why we say tonight: Private values must be at the heart of public policies.

What is true for families in America is true for America in the family of free nations. History is no captive of some inevitable force. History is made by men and women of vision and courage. Tonight freedom is on the march. The United States is the economic miracle, the model to which the world once again turns. We stand for an idea whose time is now: Only by lifting the weights from the shoulders of all can people truly prosper and can peace among all nations be secure. Teddy Roosevelt said that a nation that does great work lives forever. We have done well, but we cannot stop at the foothills when Everest beckons. It's time for America to be all that we can be.

We speak tonight of an agenda for the future, an agenda for a safer, more secure world. And we speak about the necessity for actions to steel us for the challenges of growth, trade, and security in the next decade and the year 2000. And we will do it--not by breaking faith with bedrock principles but by breaking free from failed policies. Let us begin where storm clouds loom darkest--right here in Washington, DC. This week I will send you our detailed proposals; tonight let us speak of our responsibility to redefine government's role: not to control, not to demand or command, not to contain us, but to help in times of need and, above all, to create a ladder of opportunity to full employment so that all Americans can climb toward economic power and justice on their own.

But we cannot win the race to the future shackled to a system that can't even pass a Federal budget. We cannot win that race held back by horse-and-buggy programs that waste tax dollars and squander human potential. We cannot win that race if we're swamped in a sea of red ink. Now, Mr. Speaker, you know, I know, and the American people know the Federal budget system is broken. It doesn't work. Before we leave this city, let's you and I work together to fix it, and then we can finally give the American people a balanced budget.

Members of Congress, passage of Gramm-Rudman-Hollings gives us an historic opportunity to achieve what has eluded our national leadership for decades: forcing the Federal Government to live within its means. Your schedule now requires that the budget resolution be passed by April 15th, the very day America's families have to foot the bill for the budgets that you produce. How often we read of a husband and wife both working, struggling from paycheck to paycheck to raise a family, meet a mortgage, pay their taxes and bills. And yet some in Congress say taxes must be raised. Well, I'm sorry; they're asking the wrong people to tighten their belts. It's time we reduce the Federal budget and left the family budget alone. We do not face large deficits because American families are undertaxed; we face those deficits because the Federal Government overspends.

The detailed budget that we will submit will meet the Gramm-Rudman-Hollings target for deficit reductions, meet our commitment to ensure a strong national defense, meet our commitment to protect Social Security and the truly less fortunate, and, yes, meet our commitment to not raise taxes. How should we accomplish this? Well, not by taking from those in need. As families take care of their own, government must provide shelter and nourishment for those who cannot provide for themselves. But we must revise or replace programs enacted in the name of compassion that degrade the moral worth of work, encourage family breakups, and drive entire communities into a bleak and heartless dependency. Gramm-Rudman-Hollings can mark a dramatic improvement. But experience shows that simply setting deficit targets does not assure they'll be met. We must proceed with Grace commission reforms against waste.

And tonight I ask you to give me what 43 Governors have: Give me a line-item veto this year. Give me the authority to veto waste, and I'll take the responsibility, I'll make the cuts, I'll take the heat. This authority would not give me any monopoly power, but simply prevent spending measures from sneaking through that could not pass on their own merit. And you can sustain or override my veto; that's the way the system should work. Once we've made the hard choices, we should lock in our gains with a balanced budget amendment to the Constitution.

I mentioned that we will meet our commitment to national defense. We must meet it. Defense is not just another budget expense. Keeping America strong, free, and at peace is solely the responsibility of the Federal Government; it is government's prime responsibility. We have devoted 5 years trying to narrow a dangerous gap born of illusion and neglect, and we've made important gains. Yet the threat from Soviet forces, conventional and strategic, from the Soviet drive for domination, from the increase in espionage and state terror remains great. This is reality. Closing our eyes will not make reality disappear. We pledged together to hold real growth in defense spending to the bare minimum. My budget honors that pledge, and I'm now asking you, the Congress, to keep its end of the bargain. The Soviets must know that if America reduces her defenses, it will be because of a reduced threat, not a reduced resolve.

Keeping America strong is as vital to the national security as controlling Federal spending is to our economic security. But, as I have said before, the most powerful force we can enlist against the Federal deficit is an ever-expanding American economy, unfettered and free. The magic of opportunity-unreserved, unfailing, unrestrained-isn't this the calling that unites us? I believe our tax rate cuts for the people have done more to spur a spirit of risk-taking and help America's economy break free than any program since John Kennedy's tax cut almost a quarter century ago.

Now history calls us to press on, to complete efforts for an historic tax reform providing new opportunity for all and ensuring that all pay their fair share, but no more. We've come this far. Will you join me now, and we'll walk this last mile together? You know my views on this. We cannot and we will not accept tax reform that is a tax increase in disguise. True reform must be an engine of productivity and growth, and that means a top personal rate no higher than 35 percent. True reform must be truly fair, and that means raising personal exemptions to $2,000. True reform means a tax system that at long last is profamily, projobs, profuture, and pro-America.

As we knock down the barriers to growth, we must redouble our efforts for freer and fairer trade. We have already taken actions to counter unfair trading practices and to pry open closed foreign markets. We will continue to do so. We will also oppose legislation touted as providing protection that in reality pits one American worker against another, one industry against another, one community against another, and that raises prices for us all. If the United States can trade with other nations on a level playing field, we can outproduce, outcompete, and outsell anybody, anywhere in the world.

The constant expansion of our economy and exports requires a sound and stable dollar at home and reliable exchange rates around the world. We must never again permit wild currency swings to cripple our farmers and other exporters. Farmers, in particular, have suffered from past unwise government policies. They must not be abandoned with problems they did not create and cannot control. We've begun coordinating economic and monetary policy among our major trading partners. But there's more to do, and tonight I am directing Treasury Secretary Jim Baker to determine if the nations of the world should convene to discuss the role and relationship of our currencies.

Confident in our future and secure in our values, Americans are striving forward to embrace the future. We see it not only in our recovery but in 3 straight years of falling crime rates, as families and communities band together to fight pornography, drugs, and lawlessness and to give back to their children the safe and, yes, innocent childhood they deserve. We see it in the renaissance in education, the rising SAT scores for 3 years--last year's increase, the greatest since 1963. It wasn't government and Washington lobbies that turned education around; it was the American people who, in reaching for excellence, knew to reach back to basics. We must continue the advance by supporting discipline in our schools, vouchers that give parents freedom of choice; and we must give back to our children their lost right to acknowledge God in their classrooms.

We are a nation of idealists, yet today there is a wound in our national conscience. America will never be whole as long as the right to life granted by our Creator is denied to the unborn. For the rest of my time, I shall do what I can to see that this wound is one day healed.

As we work to make the American dream real for all, we must also look to the condition of America's families. Struggling parents today worry how they will provide their children the advantages that their parents gave them. In the welfare culture, the breakdown of the family, the most basic support system, has reached crisis proportions---'m female and child poverty, child abandonment, horrible crimes, and deteriorating schools. After hundreds of billions of dollars in poverty programs, the plight of the poor grows more painful. But the waste in dollars and cents pales before the most tragic loss: the sinful waste of human spirit and potential. We can ignore this terrible truth no longer. As Franklin Roosevelt warned 51 years ago, standing before this Chamber, he said, "Welfare is a narcotic, a subtle destroyer of the human spirit." And we must now escape the spider's web of dependency.

Tonight I am charging the White House Domestic Council to present me by December 1, 1986, an evaluation of programs and a strategy for immediate action to meet the financial, educational, social, and safety concerns of poor families. I'm talking about real and lasting emancipation, because the success of welfare should be judged by how many of its recipients become independent of welfare. Further, after seeing how devastating illness can destroy the financial security of the family, I am directing the Secretary of Health and Human Services, Dr. Otis Bowen, to report to me by year end with recommendations on how the private sector and government can work together to address the problems of affordable insurance for those whose life savings would otherwise be threatened when catastrophic illness strikes.

And tonight I want to speak directly to America's younger generation, because you hold the destiny of our nation in your hands. With all the temptations young people face, it sometimes seems the allure of the permissive society requires superhuman feats of self-control. But the call of the future is too strong, the challenge too great to get lost in the blind alleyways of dissolution, drugs, and despair. Never has there been a more exciting time to be alive, a time of rousing wonder and heroic achievement. As they said in the film "Back to the Future," "Where we're going, we don't need roads."

Well, today physicists peering into the infinitely small realms of subatomic particles find reaffirmations of religious faith. Astronomers build a space telescope that can see to the edge of the universe and possibly back to the moment of creation. So, yes, this nation remains fully committed to America's space program. We're going forward with our shuttle flights. We're going forward to build our space station. And we are going forward with research on a new Orient Express that could, by the end of the next decade, take off from Dulles Airport, accelerate up to 25 times the speed of sound, attaining low Earth orbit or flying to Tokyo within 2 hours. And the same technology transforming our lives can solve the greatest problem of the 20th century. A security shield can one day render nuclear weapons obsolete and free mankind from the prison of nuclear terror. America met one historic challenge and went to the Moon. Now America must meet another: to make our strategic defense real for all the citizens of planet Earth.

Let us speak of our deepest longing for the future: to leave our children a land that is free and just and a world at peace. It is my hope that our fireside summit in Geneva and Mr. Gorbachev's upcoming visit to America can lead to a more stable relationship. Surely no people on Earth hate war or love peace more than we Americans. But we cannot stroll into the future with childlike faith. Our differences with a system that openly proclaims and practices an alleged right to command people's lives and to export its ideology by force are deep and abiding. Logic and history compel us to accept that our relationship be guided by realism--rock-hard, clear-eyed, steady, and sure. Our negotiators in Geneva have proposed a radical cut in offensive forces by each side with no cheating. They have made clear that Soviet compliance with the letter and spirit of agreements is essential. If the Soviet Government wants an agreement that truly reduces nuclear arms, there will be such an agreement.

But arms control is no substitute for peace. We know that peace follows in freedom's path and conflicts erupt when the will of the people is denied. So, we must prepare for peace not only by reducing weapons but by bolstering prosperity, liberty, and democracy however and wherever we can. We advance the promise of opportunity every time we speak out on behalf of lower tax rates, freer markets, sound currencies around the world. We strengthen the family of freedom every time we work with allies and come to the aid of friends under siege. And we can enlarge the family of free nations if we will defend the unalienable rights of all God's children to follow their dreams.

To those imprisoned in regimes held captive, to those beaten for daring to fight for freedom and democracy--for their right to worship, to speak, to live, and to prosper in the family of free nations--we say to you tonight: You are not alone, freedom fighters. America will support with moral and material assistance your right not just to fight and die for freedom but to fight and win freedom--to win freedom in Afghanistan, in Angola, in Cambodia, and in Nicaragua. This is a great moral challenge for the entire free world.

Surely no issue is more important for peace in our own hemisphere, for the security of our frontiers, for the protection of our vital interests, than to achieve democracy in Nicaragua and to protect Nicaragua's democratic neighbors. This year I will be asking Congress for the means to do what must be done for that great and good cause. As (former Senator Henry M.)Scoop Jackson, the inspiration for our Bipartisan Commission on Central America, once said, "In matters of national security, the best politics is no politics."

What we accomplish this year, in each challenge we face, will set our course for the balance of the decade, indeed, for the remainder of the century. After all we've done so far, let no one say that this nation cannot reach the destiny of our dreams. America believes, America is ready, America can win the race to the future--and we shall. The American dream is a song of hope that rings through night winter air; vivid, tender music that warms our hearts when the least among us aspire to the greatest things: to venture a daring enterprise; to unearth new beauty in music, literature, and art; to discover a new universe inside a tiny silicon chip or a single human cell.

We see the dream coming true in the spirit of discovery of Richard Cavoli. All his life he's been enthralled by the mysteries of medicine. And, Richard, we know that the experiment that you began in high school was launched and lost last week, yet your dream lives. And as long as it's real, work of noble note will yet be done, work that could reduce the harmful effects of x rays on patients and enable astronomers to view the golden gateways of the farthest stars.

We see the dream glow in the towering talent of a 12-year-old, Tyrone Ford. A child prodigy of gospel music, he has surmounted personal adversity to become an accomplished pianist and singer. He also directs the choirs of three churches and has performed at the Kennedy Center. With God as your composer, Tyrone, your music will be the music of angels.

We see the dream being saved by the courage of the 13-year-old Shelby Butler, honor student and member of her school's safety patrol. Seeing another girl freeze in terror before an out-of-control school bus, she risked her life and pulled her to safety. With bravery like yours, Shelby, America need never fear for our future.

And we see the dream born again in the joyful compassion of a 13 year old, Trevor Ferrell. Two years ago, age 11, watching men and women bedding down in abandoned doorways--on television he was watching--Trevor left his suburban Philadelphia home to bring blankets and food to the helpless and homeless. And now 250 people help him fulfill his nightly vigil. Trevor, yours is the living spirit of brotherly love.

Would you four stand up for a moment? Thank you, thank you. You are heroes of our hearts. We look at you and know it's true: In this land of dreams fulfilled, where greater dreams may be imagined, nothing is impossible, no victory is beyond our reach, no glory will ever be too great.

So, now it's up to us, all of us, to prepare America for that day when our work will pale before the greatness of America's champions in the 21st century. The world's hopes rest with America's future; America's hopes rest with us. So, let us go forward to create our world of tomorrow in faith, in unity, and in love.

God bless you, and God bless America.

NOTE: The President spoke at 8:04 p.m. in the House Chamber of the Capitol. He was introduced by Thomas P. O'Neill, Jr., Speaker of the House of Representatives. The address was broadcast live on nationwide radio and television.

State of the Union Address January 27, 1987

Mr. Speaker, Mr. President, distinguished Members of Congress, honored guests, and fellow citizens:

May I congratulate all of you who are Members of this historic 100th Congress of the United States of America. In this 200th anniversary year of our Constitution, you and I stand on the shoulders of giants--men whose words and deeds put wind in the sails of freedom. However, we must always remember that our Constitution is to be celebrated not for being old, but for being young--young with the same energy, spirit, and promise that filled each eventful day in Philadelphia's statehouse. We will be guided tonight by their acts, and we will be guided forever by their words.

Now, forgive me, but I can't resist sharing a story from those historic days. Philadelphia was bursting with civic pride in the spring of 1787, and its newspapers began embellishing the arrival of the Convention delegates with elaborate social classifications. Governors of States were called Excellency. Justices and Chancellors had reserved for them honorable with a capital "H." For Congressmen, it was honorable with a small "h." And all others were referred to as "the following respectable characters." Well, for this 100th Congress, I invoke special executive powers to declare that each of you must never be titled less than honorable with a capital "H." Incidentally, I'm delighted you are celebrating the 100th birthday of the Congress. It's always a pleasure to congratulate someone with more birthdays than I've had.

Now, there's a new face at this place of honor tonight. And please join me in warm congratulations to the Speaker of the House, Jim Wright. Mr. Speaker, you might recall a similar situation in your very first session of Congress 32 years ago. Then, as now, the speakership had changed hands and another great son of Texas, Sam Rayburn--"Mr. Sam"--sat in your chair. I cannot find better words than those used by President Eisenhower that evening. He said, "We shall have much to do together; I am sure that we will get it done and that we shall do it in harmony and good will." Tonight I renew that pledge. To you, Mr. Speaker, and to Senate Majority Leader Robert Byrd, who brings 34 years of distinguished service to the Congress, may I say: Though there are changes in the Congress, America's interests remain the same. And I am confident that, along with Republican leaders Bob Michel and Bob Dole, this Congress can make history.

Six years ago I was here to ask the Congress to join me in America's new beginning. Well, the results are something of which we can all be proud. Our inflation rate is now the lowest in a quarter of a century. The prime interest rate has fallen from the 21 1/2 percent the month before we took office to 7 1/2 percent today. And those rates have triggered the most housing starts in 8 years. The unemployment rate--still too high--is the lowest in nearly 7 years, and our people have created nearly 13 million new jobs. Over 61 percent of everyone over the age of 16, male and female, is employed--the highest percentage on record. Let's roll up our sleeves and go to work and put America's economic engine at full throttle. We can also be heartened by our progress across the world. Most important, America is at peace tonight, and freedom is on the march. And we've done much these past years to restore our defenses, our alliances, and our leadership in the world. Our sons and daughters in the services once again wear their uniforms with pride.

But though we've made much progress, I have one major regret: I took a risk with regard to our action in Iran. It did not work, and for that I assume full responsibility. The goals were worthy. I do not believe it was wrong to try to establish contacts with a country of strategic importance or to try to save lives. And certainly it was not wrong to try to secure freedom for our citizens held in barbaric captivity. But we did not achieve what we wished, and serious mistakes were made in trying to do so. We will get to the bottom of this, and I will take whatever action is called for. But in debating the past, we must not deny ourselves the successes of the future. Let it never be said of this generation of Americans that we became so obsessed with failure that we refused to take risks that could further the cause of peace and freedom in the world. Much is at stake here, and the Nation and the world are watching to see if we go forward together in the national interest or if we let partisanship weaken us. And let there be no mistake about American policy: We will not sit idly by if our interests or our friends in the Middle East are threatened, nor will we yield to terrorist blackmail.

And now, ladies and gentlemen of the Congress, why don't we get to work? I am pleased to report that because of our efforts to rebuild the strength of America, the world is a safer place. Earlier this month I submitted a budget to defend America and maintain our momentum to make up for neglect in the last decade. Well, I ask you to vote out a defense and foreign affairs budget that says yes to protecting our country. While the world is safer, it is not safe.

Since 1970 the Soviets have invested $500 billion more on their military forces than we have. Even today, though nearly 1 in 3 Soviet families is without running hot water and the average family spends 2 hours a day shopping for the basic necessities of life, their government still found the resources to transfer $75 billion in weapons to client states in the past 5 years--clients like Syria, Vietnam, Cuba, Libya, Angola, Ethiopia, Afghanistan, and Nicaragua. With 120,000 Soviet combat and military personnel and 15,000 military advisers in Asia, Africa, and Latin America, can anyone still doubt their single-minded determination to expand their power? Despite this, the Congress cut my request for critical U.S. security assistance to free nations by 21 percent this year, and cut defense requests by $85 billion in the last 3 years.

These assistance programs serve our national interests as well as mutual interests. And when the programs are devastated, American interests are harmed. My friends, it's my duty as President to say to you again tonight that there is no surer way to lose freedom than to lose our resolve. Today the brave people of Afghanistan are showing that resolve. The Soviet Union says it wants a peaceful settlement in Afghanistan, yet it continues a brutal war and props up a regime whose days are clearly numbered. We are ready to support a political solution that guarantees the rapid withdrawal of all Soviet troops and genuine self-determination for the Afghan people.

In Central America, too, the cause of freedom is being tested. And our resolve is being tested there as well. Here, especially, the world is watching to see how this nation responds. Today over 90 percent of the people of Latin America live in democracy. Democracy is on the march in Central and South America. Communist Nicaragua is the odd man out -suppressing the church, the press, and democratic dissent and promoting subversion in the region. We support diplomatic efforts, but these efforts can never succeed if the Sandinistas win their war against the Nicaraguan people.

Our commitment to a Western Hemisphere safe from aggression did not occur by spontaneous generation on the day that we took office. It began with the Monroe Doctrine in 1823 and continues our historic bipartisan American policy. Franklin Roosevelt said we "are determined to do everything possible to maintain peace on this hemisphere." President Truman was very blunt: "International communism seeks to crush and undermine and destroy the independence of the Americas. We cannot let that happen here." And John F. Kennedy made clear that "Communist domination in this hemisphere can never be negotiated." Some in this Congress may choose to depart from this historic commitment, but I will not.

This year we celebrate the second century of our Constitution. The Sandinistas just signed theirs 2 weeks ago, and then suspended it. We won't know how my words tonight will be reported there for one simple reason: There is no free press in Nicaragua. Nicaraguan freedom fighters have never asked us to wage their battle, but I will fight any effort to shut off their lifeblood and consign them to death, defeat, or a life without freedom. There must be no Soviet beachhead in Central America.

You know, we Americans have always preferred dialog to conflict, and so, we always remain open to more constructive relations with the Soviet Union. But more responsible Soviet conduct around the world is a key element of the U.S.-Soviet agenda. Progress is also required on the other items of our agenda as well--real respect for human rights and more open contacts between our societies and, of course, arms reduction.

In Iceland, last October, we had one moment of opportunity that the Soviets dashed because they sought to cripple our Strategic Defense Initiative, SDI. I wouldn't let them do it then; I won't let them do it now or in the future. This is the most positive and promising defense program we have undertaken. It's the path, for both sides, to a safer future--a system that defends human life instead of threatening it. SDI will go forward. The United States has made serious, fair, and far-reaching proposals to the Soviet Union, and this is a moment of rare opportunity for arms reduction. But I will need, and American negotiators in Geneva will need, Congress' support. Enacting the Soviet negotiating position into American law would not be the way to win a good agreement. So, I must tell you in this Congress I will veto any effort that undercuts our national security and our negotiating leverage.

Now, today, we also find ourselves engaged in expanding peaceful commerce across the world. We will work to expand our opportunities in international markets through the Uruguay round of trade negotiations and to complete an historic free trade arrangement between the world's two largest trading partners, Canada and the United States. Our basic trade policy remains the same: We remain opposed as ever to protectionism, because America's growth and future depend on trade. But we would insist on trade that is fair and free. We are always willing to be trade partners but never trade patsies.

Now, from foreign borders let us return to our own, because America in the world is only as strong as America at home. This 100th Congress has high responsibilities. I begin with a gentle reminder that many of these are simply the incomplete obligations of the past. The American people deserve to be impatient, because we do not yet have the public house in order. We've had great success in restoring our economic integrity, and we've rescued our nation from the worst economic mess since the Depression. But there's more to do. For starters, the Federal deficit is outrageous. For years I've asked that we stop pushing onto our children the excesses of our government. And what the Congress finally needs to do is pass a constitutional amendment that mandates a balanced budget and forces government to live within its means. States, cities, and the families of America balance their budgets. Why can't we?

Next, the budget process is a sorry spectacle. The missing of deadlines and the nightmare of monstrous continuing resolutions packing hundreds of billions of dollars of spending into one bill must be stopped. We ask the Congress once again: Give us the same tool that 43 Governors have--a line-item veto so we can carve out the boondoggles and pork, those items that would never survive on their own. I will send the Congress broad recommendations on the budget, but first I'd like to see yours. Let's go to work and get this done together.

But now let's talk about this year's budget. Even though I have submitted it within the Gramm-Rudman-Hollings deficit reduction target, I have seen suggestions that we might postpone that timetable. Well, I think the American people are tired of hearing the same old excuses. Together we made a commitment to balance the budget. Now let's keep it. As for those suggestions that the answer is higher taxes, the American people have repeatedly rejected that shop-worn advice. They know that we don't have deficits because people are taxed too little. We have deficits because big government spends too much.

Now, next month I'll place two additional reforms before the Congress. We've created a welfare monster that is a shocking indictment of our sense of priorities. Our national welfare system consists of some 59 major programs and over 6,000 pages of Federal laws and regulations on which more than $132 billion was spent in 1985. I will propose a new national welfare strategy, a program of welfare reform through State-sponsored, community-based demonstration projects. This is the time to reform this outmoded social dinosaur and finally break the poverty trap. Now, we will never abandon those who, through no fault of their own, must have our help. But let us work to see how many can be freed from the dependency of welfare and made self-supporting, which the great majority of welfare recipients want more than anything else. Next, let us remove a financial specter facing our older Americans: the fear of an illness so expensive that it can result in having to make an intolerable choice between bankruptcy and death. I will submit legislation shortly to help free the elderly from the fear of catastrophic illness.

Now let's turn to the future. It's widely said that America is losing her competitive edge. Well, that won't happen if we act now. How well prepared are we to enter the 21st century? In my lifetime, America set the standard for the world. It is now time to determine that we should enter the next century having achieved a level of excellence unsurpassed in history. We will achieve this, first, by guaranteeing that government does everything possible to promote America's ability to compete. Second, we must act as individuals in a quest for excellence that will not be measured by new proposals or billions in new funding. Rather, it involves an expenditure of American spirit and just plain American grit. The Congress will soon receive my comprehensive proposals to enhance our competitiveness, including new science and technology centers and strong new funding for basic research. The bill will include legal and regulatory reforms and weapons to fight unfair trade practices. Competitiveness also means giving our farmers a shot at participating fairly and fully in a changing world market.

Preparing for the future must begin, as always, with our children. We need to set for them new and more rigorous goals. We must demand more of ourselves and our children by raising literacy levels dramatically by the year 2000. Our children should master the basic concepts of math and science, and let's insist that students not leave high school until they have studied and understood the basic documents of our national heritage. There's one more thing we can't let up on: Let's redouble our personal efforts to provide for every child a safe and drug-free learning environment. If our crusade against drugs succeeds with our children, we will defeat that scourge all over the country.

Finally, let's stop suppressing the spiritual core of our national being. Our nation could not have been conceived without divine help. Why is it that we can build a nation with our prayers, but we can't use a schoolroom for voluntary prayer? The 100th Congress of the United States should be remembered as the one that ended the expulsion of God from America's classrooms.

The quest for excellence into the 21st century begins in the schoolroom but must go next to the workplace. More than 20 million new jobs will be created before the new century unfolds, and by then, our economy should be able to provide a job for everyone who wants to work. We must also enable our workers to adapt to the rapidly changing nature of the workplace. And I will propose substantial, new Federal commitments keyed to retraining and job mobility.

Over the next few weeks, I'll be sending the Congress a complete series of these special messages--on budget reform, welfare reform, competitiveness, including education, trade, worker training and assistance, agriculture, and other subjects. The Congress can give us these tools, but to make these tools work, it really comes down to just being our best. And that is the core of American greatness. The responsibility of freedom presses us towards higher knowledge and, I believe, moral and spiritual greatness. Through lower taxes and smaller government, government has its ways of freeing people's spirits. But only we, each of us, can let the spirit soar against our own individual standards. Excellence is what makes freedom ring. And isn't that what we do best?

We're entering our third century now, but it's wrong to judge our nation by its years. The calendar can't measure America because we were meant to be an endless experiment in freedom--with no limit to our reaches, no boundaries to what we can do, no end point to our hopes. The United States Constitution is the impassioned and inspired vehicle by which we travel through history. It grew out of the most fundamental inspiration of our existence: that we are here to serve Him by living free--that living free releases in us the noblest of impulses and the best of our abilities; that we would use these gifts for good and generous purposes and would secure them not just for ourselves and for our children but for all mankind.

Over the years--I won't count if you don't--nothing has been so heartwarming to me as speaking to America's young, and the little ones especially, so fresh-faced and so eager to know. Well, from time to time I've been with them--they will ask about our Constitution. And I hope you Members of Congress will not deem this a breach of protocol if you'll permit me to share these thoughts again with the young people who might be listening or watching this evening. I've read the constitutions of a number of countries, including the Soviet Union's. Now, some people are surprised to hear that they have a constitution, and it even supposedly grants a number of freedoms to its people. Many countries have written into their constitution provisions for freedom of speech and freedom of assembly. Well, if this is true, why is the Constitution of the United States so exceptional?

Well, the difference is so small that it almost escapes you, but it's so great it tells you the whole story in just three words: We the people. In those other constitutions, the Government tells the people of those countries what they're allowed to do. In our Constitution, we the people tell the Government what it can do, and it can do only those things listed in that document and no others. Virtually every other revolution in history has just exchanged one set of rulers for another set of rulers. Our revolution is the first to say the people are the masters and government is their servant. And you young people out there, don't ever forget that. Someday you could be in this room, but wherever you are, America is depending on you to reach your highest and be your best--because here in America, we the people are in charge.

Just three words: We the people--those are the kids on Christmas Day looking out from a frozen sentry post on the 38th parallel in Korea or aboard an aircraft carrier in the Mediterranean. A million miles from home, but doing their duty.

We the people--those are the warmhearted whose numbers we can't begin to count, who'll begin the day with a little prayer for hostages they will never know and MIA families they will never meet. Why? Because that's the way we are, this unique breed we call Americans.

We the people--they're farmers on tough times, but who never stop feeding a hungry world. They're the volunteers at the hospital choking back their tears for the hundredth time, caring for a baby struggling for life because of a mother who used drugs. And you'll forgive me a special memory--it's a million mothers like Nelle Reagan who never knew a stranger or turned a hungry person away from her kitchen door.

We the people--they refute last week's television commentary downgrading our optimism and our idealism. They are the entrepreneurs, the builders, the pioneers, and a lot of regular folks--the true heroes of our land who make up the most uncommon nation of doers in history. You know they're Americans because their spirit is as big as the universe and their hearts are bigger than their spirits.

We the people--starting the third century of a dream and standing up to some cynic who's trying to tell us we're not going to get any better. Are we at the end? Well, I can't tell it any better than the real thing--a story recorded by James Madison from the final moments of the Constitutional Convention, September 17th, 1787. As the last few members signed the document, Benjamin Franklin--the oldest delegate at 81 years and in frail health--looked over toward the chair where George Washington daily presided. At the back of the chair was painted the picture of a Sun on the horizon. And turning to those sitting next to him, Franklin observed that artists found it difficult in their painting to distinguish between a rising and a setting Sun.

Well, I know if we were there, we could see those delegates sitting around Franklin-leaning in to listen more closely to him. And then Dr. Franklin began to share his deepest hopes and fears about the outcome of their efforts, and this is what he said: "I have often looked at that picture behind the President without being able to tell whether it was a rising or setting Sun: But now at length I have the happiness to know that it is a rising and not a setting Sun." Well, you can bet it's rising because, my fellow citizens, America isn't finished. Her best days have just begun.

Thank you, God bless you, and God bless America.

NOTE: The President spoke at 9:03 p.m. in the House Chamber of the Capitol. He was introduced by Jim Wright, Speaker of the House of Representatives. The address was broadcast live on nationwide radio and television.

State of the Union Address January 25, 1988

Mr. Speaker, Mr. President, and distinguished Members of the House and Senate: When we first met here 7 years ago-many of us for the first time--it was with the hope of beginning something new for America. We meet here tonight in this historic Chamber to continue that work. If anyone expects just a proud recitation of the accomplishments of my administration, I say let's leave that to history; we're not finished yet. So, my message to you tonight is put on your work shoes; we're still on the job.

History records the power of the ideas that brought us here those 7 years ago-ideas like the individual's right to reach as far and as high as his or her talents will permit; the free market as an engine of economic progress. And as an ancient Chinese philosopher, Lao-tzu, said: "Govern a great nation as you would cook a small fish; do not overdo it." Well, these ideas were part of a larger notion, a vision, if you will, of America herself---an America not only rich in opportunity for the individual but an America, too, of strong families and vibrant neighborhoods; an America whose divergent but harmonizing communities were a reflection of a deeper community of values: the value of work, of family, of religion, and of the love of freedom that God places in each of us and whose defense He has entrusted in a special way to this nation.

All of this was made possible by an idea I spoke of when Mr. Gorbachev was here-the belief that the most exciting revolution ever known to humankind began with three simple words: "We the People," the revolutionary notion that the people grant government its rights, and not the other way around. And there's one lesson that has come home powerfully to me, which I would offer to you now. Just as those who created this Republic pledged to each other their lives, their fortunes, and their sacred honor, so, too, America's leaders today must pledge to each other that we will keep foremost in our hearts and minds not what is best for ourselves or for our party but what is best for America.

In the spirit of Jefferson, let us affirm that in this Chamber tonight there are no Republicans, no Democrats--just Americans. Yes, we will have our differences, but let us always remember what unites us far outweighs whatever divides us. Those who sent us here to serve them--the millions of Americans watching and listening tonight-expect this of us. Let's prove to them and to ourselves that democracy works even in an election year. We've done this before. And as we have worked together to bring down spending, tax rates, and inflation, employment has climbed to record heights; America has created more jobs and better, higher paying jobs; family income has risen for 4 straight years, and America's poor climbed out of poverty at the fastest rate in more than 10 years.

Our record is not just the longest peacetime expansion in history but an economic and social revolution of hope based on work, incentives, growth, and opportunity; a revolution of compassion that led to private sector initiatives and a 77-percent increase in charitable giving; a revolution that at a critical moment in world history reclaimed and restored the American dream.

In international relations, too, there's only one description for what, together, we have achieved: a complete turnabout, a revolution. Seven years ago, America was weak, and freedom everywhere was under siege. Today America is strong, and democracy is everywhere on the move. From Central America to East Asia, ideas like free markets and democratic reforms and human rights are taking hold. We've replaced "Blame America" with "Look up to America." We've rebuilt our defenses. And of all our accomplishments, none can give us more satisfaction than knowing that our young people are again proud to wear our country's uniform.

And in a few moments, I'm going to talk about three developments--arms reduction, the Strategic Defense Initiative, and the global democratic revolution--that, when taken together, offer a chance none of us would have dared imagine 7 years ago, a chance to rid the world of the two great nightmares of the postwar era. I speak of the startling hope of giving our children a future free of both totalitarianism and nuclear terror.

Tonight, then, we're strong, prosperous, at peace, and we are free. This is the state of our Union. And if we will work together this year, I believe we can give a future President and a future Congress the chance to make that prosperity, that peace, that freedom not just the state of our Union but the state of our world.

Toward this end, we have four basic objectives tonight. First, steps we can take this year to keep our economy strong and growing, to give our children a future of low inflation and full employment. Second, let's check our progress in attacking social problems, where important gains have been made, but which still need critical attention. I mean schools that work, economic independence for the poor, restoring respect for family life and family values. Our third objective tonight is global: continuing the exciting economic and democratic revolutions we've seen around the world. Fourth and finally, our nation has remained at peace for nearly a decade and a half, as we move toward our goals of world prosperity and world freedom. We must protect that peace and deter war by making sure the next President inherits what you and I have a moral obligation to give that President: a national security that is unassailable and a national defense that takes full advantage of new technology and is fully funded.

This is a full agenda. It's meant to be. You see, my thinking on the next year is quite simple: Let's make this the best of 8. And that means it's all out--right to the finish line. I don't buy the idea that this is the last year of anything, because we're not talking here tonight about registering temporary gains but ways of making permanent our successes. And that's why our focus is the values, the principles, and ideas that made America great. Let's be clear on this point. We're for limited government, because we understand, as the Founding Fathers did, that it is the best way of ensuring personal liberty and empowering the individual so that every American of every race and region shares fully in the flowering of American prosperity and freedom.

One other thing we Americans like--the future--like the sound of it, the idea of it, the hope of it. Where others fear trade and economic growth, we see opportunities for creating new wealth and undreamed-of opportunities for millions in our own land and beyond. Where others seek to throw up barriers, we seek to bring them down. Where others take counsel of their fears, we follow our hopes. Yes, we Americans like the future and like making the most of it. Let's do that now.

And let's begin by discussing how to maintain economic growth by controlling and eventually eliminating the problem of Federal deficits. We have had a balanced budget only eight times in the last 57 years. For the first time in 14 years, the Federal Government spent less in real terms last year than the year before. We took $73 billion off last year's deficit compared to the year before. The deficit itself has moved from 6.3 percent of the gross national product to only 3.4 percent. And perhaps the most important sign of progress has been the change in our view of deficits. You know, a few of us can remember when, not too many years ago, those who created the deficits said they would make us prosperous and not to worry about the debt, because we owe it to ourselves. Well, at last there is agreement that we can't spend ourselves rich.

Our recent budget agreement, designed to reduce Federal deficits by $76 billion over the next 2 years, builds on this consensus. But this agreement must be adhered to without slipping into the errors of the past: more broken promises and more unchecked spending. As I indicated in my first State of the Union, what ails us can be simply put: The Federal Government is too big, and it spends too much money. I can assure you, the bipartisan leadership of Congress, of my help in fighting off any attempt to bust our budget agreement. And this includes the swift and certain use of the veto power.

Now, it's also time for some plain talk about the most immediate obstacle to controlling Federal deficits. The simple but frustrating problem of making expenses match revenues--something American families do and the Federal Government can't--has caused crisis after crisis in this city. Mr. Speaker, Mr. President, I will say to you tonight what I have said before and will continue to say: The budget process has broken down; it needs a drastic overhaul. With each ensuing year, the spectacle before the American people is the same as it was this Christmas: budget deadlines delayed or missed completely, monstrous continuing resolutions that pack hundreds of billions of dollars worth of spending into one bill, and a Federal Government on the brink of default.

I know I'm echoing what you here in the Congress have said, because you suffered so directly. But let's recall that in 7 years, of 91 appropriations bills scheduled to arrive on my desk by a certain date, only 10 made it on time. Last year, of the 13 appropriations bills due by October 1st, none of them made it. Instead, we had four continuing resolutions lasting 41 days, then 36 days, and 2 days, and 3 days, respectively.

And then, along came these behemoths. This is the conference report--1,053 pages, report weighing 14 pounds. Then this--a reconciliation bill 6 months late that was 1,186 pages long, weighing 15 pounds. And the long-term continuing resolution--this one was 2 months late, and it's 1,057 pages long, weighing 14 pounds. That was a total of 43 pounds of paper and ink. You had 3 hours--yes, 3 hours--to consider each, and it took 300 people at my Office of Management and Budget just to read the bill so the Government wouldn't shut down. Congress shouldn't send another one of these. No, and if you do, I will not sign it.

Let's change all this. Instead of a Presidential budget that gets discarded and a congressional budget resolution that is not enforced, why not a simple partnership, a joint agreement that sets out the spending priorities within the available revenues? And let's remember our deadline is October 1st, not Christmas. Let's get the people's work done in time to avoid a footrace with Santa Claus. And, yes, this year--to coin a phrase--a new beginning: 13 individual bills, on time and fully reviewed by Congress.

I'm also certain you join me in saying: Let's help ensure our future of prosperity by giving the President a tool that, though I will not get to use it, is one I know future Presidents of either party must have. Give the President the same authority that 43 Governors use in their States: the right to reach into massive appropriation bills, pare away the waste, and enforce budget discipline. Let's approve the line-item veto.

And let's take a partial step in this direction. Most of you in this Chamber didn't know what was in this catchall bill and report. Over the past few weeks, we've all learned what was tucked away behind a little comma here and there. For example, there's millions for items such as cranberry research, blueberry research, the study of crawfish, and the commercialization of wildflowers. And that's not to mention the five or so million ($.5 million) that--so that people from developing nations could come here to watch Congress at work. I won't even touch that. So, tonight I offer you this challenge. In 30 days I will send back to you those items as rescissions, which if I had the authority to line them out I would do so.

Now, review this multibillion-dollar package that will not undercut our bipartisan budget agreement. As a matter of fact, if adopted, it will improve our deficit reduction goals. And what an example we can set, that we're serious about getting our financial accounts in order. By acting and approving this plan, you have the opportunity to override a congressional process that is out of control.

There is another vital reform. Yes, Gramm-Rudman-Hollings has been profoundly helpful, but let us take its goal of a balanced budget and make it permanent. Let us do now what so many States do to hold down spending and what 32 State legislatures have asked us to do. Let us heed the wishes of an overwhelming plurality of Americans and pass a constitutional amendment that mandates a balanced budget and forces the Federal Government to live within its means. Reform of the budget process--including the line-item veto and balanced budget amendment--will, together with real restraint on government spending, prevent the Federal budget from ever again ravaging the family budget.

Let's ensure that the Federal Government never again legislates against the family and the home. Last September 1 signed an Executive order on the family requiring that every department and agency review its activities in light of seven standards designed to promote and not harm the family. But let us make certain that the family is always at the center of the public policy process not just in this administration but in all future administrations. It's time for Congress to consider, at the beginning, a statement of the impact that legislation will have on the basic unit of American society, the family.

And speaking of the family, let's turn to a matter on the mind of every American parent tonight: education. We all know the sorry story of the sixties and seventies-soaring spending, plummeting test scores-and that hopeful trend of the eighties, when we replaced an obsession with dollars with a commitment to quality, and test scores started back up. There's a lesson here that we all should write on the blackboard a hundred times: In a child's education, money can never take the place of basics like discipline, hard work, and, yes, homework.

As a nation we do, of course, spend heavily on education--more than we spend on defense. Yet across our country, Governors like New Jersey's Tom Kean are giving classroom demonstrations that how we spend is as important as how much we spend. Opening up the teaching profession to all qualified candidates, merit pay--so that good teachers get

A's as well as apples--and stronger curriculum, as Secretary Bennett has proposed for high schools--these imaginative reforms are making common sense the most popular new kid in America's schools. How can we help? Well, we can talk about and push for these reforms. But the most important thing we can do is to reaffirm that control of our schools belongs to the States, local communities and, most of all, to the parents and teachers.

My friends, some years ago, the Federal Government declared war on poverty, and poverty won. Today the Federal Government has 59 major welfare programs and spends more than $100 billion a year on them. What has all this money done? Well, too often it has only made poverty harder to escape. Federal welfare programs have created a massive social problem. With the best of intentions, government created a poverty trap that wreaks havoc on the very support system the poor need most to lift themselves out of poverty: the family. Dependency has become the one enduring heirloom, passed from one generation to the next, of too many fragmented families.

It is time--this may be the most radical thing I've said in 7 years in this office--it's time for Washington to show a little humility. There are a thousand sparks of genius in 50 States and a thousand communities around the Nation. It is time to nurture them and see which ones can catch fire and become guiding lights. States have begun to show us the way. They've demonstrated that successful welfare programs can be built around more effective child support enforcement practices and innovative programs requiring welfare recipients to work or prepare for work. Let us give the States more flexibility and encourage more reforms. Let's start making our welfare system the first rung on America's ladder of opportunity, a boost up from dependency, not a graveyard but a birthplace of hope.

And now let me turn to three other matters vital to family values and the quality of family life. The first is an untold American success story. Recently, we released our annual survey of what graduating high school seniors have to say about drugs. Cocaine use is declining, and marijuana use was the lowest since surveying began. We can be proud that our students are just saying no to drugs. But let us remember what this menace requires: commitment from every part of America and every single American, a commitment to a drugfree America. The war against drugs is a war of individual battles, a crusade with many heroes, including America's young people and also someone very special to me. She has helped so many of our young people to say no to drugs. Nancy, much credit belongs to you, and I want to express to you your husband's pride and your country's thanks.'. Surprised you, didn't I?

Well, now we come to a family issue that we must have the courage to confront. Tonight, I call America--a good nation, a moral people--to charitable but realistic consideration of the terrible cost of abortion on demand. To those who say this violates a woman's right to control of her own body: Can they deny that now medical evidence confirms the unborn child is a living human being entitled to life, liberty, and the pursuit of happiness? Let us unite as a nation and protect the unborn with legislation that would stop all Federal funding for abortion and with a human life amendment making, of course, an exception where the unborn child threatens the life of the mother. Our Judeo-Christian tradition recognizes the right of taking a life in self-defense. But with that one exception, let us look to those others in our land who cry out for children to adopt. I pledge to you tonight I will work to remove barriers to adoption and extend full sharing in family life to millions of Americans so that children who need homes can be welcomed to families who want them and love them.

And let me add here: So many of our greatest statesmen have reminded us that spiritual values alone are essential to our nation's health and vigor. The Congress opens its proceedings each day, as does the Supreme Court, with an acknowledgment of the Supreme Being. Yet we are denied the right to set aside in our schools a moment each day for those who wish to pray. I believe Congress should pass our school prayer amendment.

Now, to make sure there is a full nine member Supreme Court to interpret the law, to protect the rights of all Americans, I urge the Senate to move quickly and decisively in confirming Judge Anthony Kennedy to the highest Court in the land and to also confirm 27 nominees now waiting to fill vacancies in the Federal judiciary.

Here then are our domestic priorities. Yet if the Congress and the administration work together, even greater opportunities lie ahead to expand a growing world economy, to continue to reduce the threat of nuclear arms, and to extend the frontiers of freedom and the growth of democratic institutions.

Our policies consistently received the strongest support of the late Congressman Dan Daniel of Virginia. I'm sure all of you join me in expressing heartfelt condolences on his passing.

One of the greatest contributions the United States can make to the world is to promote freedom as the key to economic growth. A creative, competitive America is the answer to a changing world, not trade wars that would close doors, create greater barriers, and destroy millions of jobs. We should always remember: Protectionism is destructionism. America's jobs, America's growth, America's future depend on trade--trade that is free, open, and fair.

This year, we have it within our power to take a major step toward a growing global economy and an expanding cycle of prosperity that reaches to all the free nations of this Earth. I'm speaking of the historic free trade agreement negotiated between our country and Canada. And I can also tell you that we're determined to expand this concept, south as well as north. Next month I will be traveling to Mexico, where trade matters will be of foremost concern. And over the next several months, our Congress and the Canadian Parliament can make the start of such a North American accord a reality. Our goal must be a day when the free flow of trade, from the tip of Tierra del Fuego to the Arctic Circle, unites the people of the Western Hemisphere in a bond of mutually beneficial exchange, when all borders become what the U.S.-Canadian border so long has been: a meeting place rather than a dividing line.

This movement we see in so many places toward economic freedom is indivisible from the worldwide movement toward political freedom and against totalitarian rule. This global democratic revolution has removed the specter, so frightening a decade ago, of democracy doomed to permanent minority status in the world. In South and Central America, only a third of the people enjoyed democratic rule in 1976. Today over 90 percent of Latin Americans live in nations committed to democratic principles. And the resurgence of democracy is owed to these courageous people on almost every continent who have struggled to take control of their own destiny.

In Nicaragua the struggle has extra meaning, because that nation is so near our own borders. The recent revelations of a former high-level Sandinista major, Roger Miranda, show us that, even as they talk peace, the Communist Sandinista government of Nicaragua has established plans for a large 600,000-man army. Yet even as these plans are made, the Sandinista regime knows the tide is turning, and the cause of Nicaraguan freedom is riding at its crest. Because of the freedom fighters, who are resisting Communist rule, the Sandinistas have been forced to extend some democratic rights, negotiate with church authorities, and release a few political prisoners.

The focus is on the Sandinistas, their promises and their actions. There is a consensus among the four Central American democratic Presidents that the Sandinistas have not complied with the plan to bring peace and democracy to all of Central America. The Sandinistas again have promised reforms. Their challenge is to take irreversible steps toward democracy. On Wednesday my request to sustain the freedom fighters will be submitted, which reflects our mutual desire for peace, freedom, and democracy in Nicaragua. I ask

Congress to pass this request. Let us be for the people of Nicaragua what Lafayette, Pulaski, and Von Steuben were for our forefathers and the cause of American independence.

So, too, in Afghanistan, the freedom fighters are the key to peace. We support the Mujahidin. There can be no settlement unless all Soviet troops are removed and the Afghan people are allowed genuine self-determination. I have made my views on this matter known to Mr. Gorbachev. But not just Nicaragua or Afghanistan--yes, everywhere we see a swelling freedom tide across the world: freedom fighters rising up in Cambodia and Angola, fighting and dying for the same democratic liberties we hold sacred. Their cause is our cause: freedom.

Yet even as we work to expand world freedom, we must build a safer peace and reduce the danger of nuclear war. But let's have no illusions. Three years of steady decline in the value of our annual defense investment have increased the risk of our most basic security interests, jeopardizing earlier hard-won goals. We must face squarely the implications of this negative trend and make adequate, stable defense spending a top goal both this year and in the future.

This same concern applies to economic and security assistance programs as well. But the resolve of America and its NATO allies has opened the way for unprecedented achievement in arms reduction. Our recently signed INF treaty is historic, because it reduces nuclear arms and establishes the most stringent verification regime in arms control history, including several forms of short-notice, on-site inspection. I submitted the treaty today, and I urge the Senate to give its advice and consent to ratification of this landmark agreement. Thank you very much.

In addition to the INF treaty, we're within reach of an even more significant START agreement that will reduce U.S. and Soviet long-range missile--or strategic arsenals by half. But let me be clear. Our approach is not to seek agreement for agreement's sake but to settle only for agreements that truly enhance our national security and that of our allies. We will never put our security at risk--or that of our allies-just to reach an agreement with the Soviets. No agreement is better than a bad agreement.

As I mentioned earlier, our efforts are to give future generations what we never had--a future free of nuclear terror. Reduction of strategic offensive arms is one step, SDI another. Our funding request for our Strategic Defense Initiative is less than 2 percent of the total defense budget. SDI funding is money wisely appropriated and money well spent. SDI has the same purpose and supports the same goals of arms reduction. It reduces the risk of war and the threat of nuclear weapons to all mankind. Strategic defenses that threaten no one could offer the world a safer, more stable basis for deterrence. We must also remember that SDI is our insurance policy against a nuclear accident, a Chernobyl of the sky, or an accidental launch or some madman who might come along.

We've seen such changes in the world in 7 years. As totalitarianism struggles to avoid being overwhelmed by the forces of economic advance and the aspiration for human freedom, it is the free nations that are resilient and resurgent. As the global democratic revolution has put totalitarianism on the defensive, we have left behind the days of retreat. America is again a vigorous leader of the free world, a nation that acts decisively and firmly in the furtherance of her principles and vital interests. No legacy would make me more proud than leaving in place a bipartisan consensus for the cause of world freedom, a consensus that prevents a paralysis of American power from ever occurring again.

But my thoughts tonight go beyond this, and I hope you'll let me end this evening with a personal reflection. You know, the world could never be quite the same again after Jacob Shallus, a trustworthy and dependable clerk of the Pennsylvania General Assembly, took his pen and engrossed those words about representative government in the preamble of our Constitution. And in a quiet but final way, the course of human events was forever altered when, on a ridge overlooking the Emmitsburg Pike in an obscure Pennsylvania town called Gettysburg, Lincoln spoke of our duty to government of and by the people and never letting it perish from the Earth.

At the start of this decade, I suggested that we live in equally momentous times, that it is up to us now to decide whether our form of government would endure and whether history still had a place of greatness for a quiet, pleasant, greening land called America. Not everything has been made perfect in 7 years, nor will it be made perfect in seven times 70 years, but before us, this year and beyond, are great prospects for the cause of peace and world freedom.

It means, too, that the young Americans I spoke of 7 years ago, as well as those who might be coming along the Virginia or Maryland shores this night and seeing for the first time the lights of this Capital City--the lights that cast their glow on our great halls of government and the monuments to the memory of our great men--it means those young Americans will find a city of hope in a land that is free.

We can be proud that for them and for us, as those lights along the Potomac are still seen this night signaling as they have for nearly two centuries and as we pray God they always will, that another generation of Americans has protected and passed on lovingly this place called America, this shining city on a hill, this government of, by, and for the people.

Thank you, and God bless you.

NOTE: The President spoke at 9:07 p.m. in the House Chamber of the Capitol. He was introduced by Jim Wright, Speaker of the House of Representatives. The address was broadcast live on nationwide radio and television.

THE CONSTITUTION OF THE UNITED STATES OF AMERICA, 1787

We the people of the United States, in Order to form a more perfect Union, establish Justice, insure domestic Tranquility, provide for the common defence, promote the general Welfare, and secure the Blessings of Liberty to ourselves and our Posterity, do ordain and establish this Constitution for the United States of America.

ARTICLE I

Section 1. All legislative Powers herein granted shall be vested in a Congress of the United States, which shall consist of a Senate and House of Representatives.

Section 2. The House of Representatives shall be composed of Members chosen every second Year by the People of the several States, and the electors in each State shall have the qualifications requisite for electors of the most numerous branch of the State legislature.

No Person shall be a Representative who shall not have attained to the Age of twenty five Years, and been seven Years a citizen of the United States, and who shall not, when elected, be an Inhabitant of that State in which he shall be chosen.

Representatives and direct Taxes shall be apportioned among the several States which may be included within this Union, according to their respective Numbers, which shall be determined by adding to the whole number of free Persons, including those bound to Service for a Term of Years, and excluding Indians not taxed, three fifths of all other Persons. The actual Enumeration shall be made within three Years after the first Meeting of the Congress of the United

States, and within every subsequent Term of ten Years, in such Manner as they shall by law Direct. The number of Representatives shall not exceed one for every thirty Thousand, but each State shall have at least one Representative; and until such enumeration shall be made, the State of New Hampshire shall be entitled to chuse three, Massachusetts eight, Rhode Island and Providence Plantations one, Connecticut five, New York six, New Jersey four, Pennsylvania eight, Delaware one, Maryland six, Virginia ten, North Carolina five, South Carolina five, and Georgia three.

When vacancies happen in the Representation from any State, the Executive Authority thereof shall issue Writs of Election to fill such Vacancies.

The House of Representatives shall chuse their Speaker and other Officers; and shall have the sole Power of Impeachment.

Section 3. The Senate of the United States shall be composed of two Senators from each State, chosen by the legislature thereof, for six Years; and each Senator shall have one Vote.

Immediately after they shall be assembled in Consequence of the first Election, they shall be divided as equally as may be into three Classes. The Seats of the Senators of the first Class shall be vacated at the expiration of the second Year, of the second Class at the expiration of the fourth Year, and of the third Class at the expiration of the sixth Year, so that one third may be chosen every second Year; and if vacancies happen by Resignation, or otherwise, during the recess of the Legislature of any State, the Executive thereof may make temporary Appointments until the next meeting of the Legislature, which shall then fill such Vacancies.

No person shall be a Senator who shall not have attained to the Age of thirty Years, and been nine Years a Citizen of the United States, and who shall not, when elected, be an Inhabitant of that State for which he shall be chosen.

The Vice-President of the United States shall be President

of the Senate, but shall have no Vote, unless they be equally divided.

The Senate shall choose their other Officers, and also a President pro tempore, in the Absence of the Vice-President, or when he shall exercise the Office of President of the United States.

The Senate shall have the sole Power to try all Impeachments. When sitting for that Purpose, they shall be on Oath or Affirmation. When the President of the United States is tried, the Chief Justice shall preside: And no Person shall be convicted without the Concurrence of two thirds of the Members present.

Judgment in cases of Impeachment shall not extend further than to removal from Office, and disqualification to hold and enjoy any Office of honor, Trust or Profit under the United States: but the Party convicted shall nevertheless be liable and subject to Indictment, Trial, Judgment and Punishment, according to Law.

Section 4. The Times, Places and Manner of holding Elections for Senators and Representatives, shall be prescribed in each State by the Legislature thereof; but the Congress may at any time by Law make or alter such Regulations, except as to the Places of chusing Senators.

The Congress shall assemble at least once in every Year, and such Meeting shall be on the first Monday in December, unless they shall by law appoint a different Day.

Section 5. Each House shall be the Judge of the Elections, Returns and Qualifications of its own Members, and a Majority of each shall constitute a Quorum to do Business; but a smaller Number may adjourn from day to day, and may be authorized to compel the Attendance of absent Members, in such Manner, and under such Penalties as each House may provide.

Each house may determine the Rules of its Proceedings, punish its Members for disorderly Behavior, and, with the Concurrence of two-thirds, expel a Member.

Each house shall keep a Journal of its Proceedings, and from time to time publish the same, excepting such Parts as may in their Judgment require Secrecy; and the Yeas and Nays of the Members of either House on any question shall, at the Desire of one fifth of those Present, be entered on the Journal.

Neither House, during the Session of Congress, shall, without the Consent of the other, adjourn for more than three days, nor to any other Place than that in which the two Houses shall be sitting.

Section 6. The Senators and Representatives shall receive a Compensation for their Services, to be ascertained by Law, and paid out of the Treasury of the United States. They shall in all Cases, except Treason, Felony and Breach of the Peace, be privileged from Arrest during their Attendance at the Session of their respective Houses, and in going to and returning from the same; and for any Speech or Debate in either House, they shall not be questioned in any other Place.

No Senator or Representative shall, during the Time for which he was elected, be appointed to any civil Office under the authority of the United States, which shall have been created, or the Emoluments whereof shall have been increased during such time; and no Person holding any Office under the United States, shall be a Member of either House during his Continuance in Office.

Section 7. All Bills for raising Revenue shall originate in the House of Representatives; but the Senate may propose or concur with Amendments as on other Bills.

Every Bill which shall have passed the House of Representatives and the Senate, shall, before it become a Law, be presented to the President of the United States; If he approve he shall sign it, but if not he shall return it, with his Objections to that House in which it shall have originated, who shall enter the Objections at large on their Journal, and proceed to reconsider it. If after such Reconsideration two thirds of that house shall agree to pass the Bill, it shall be sent, together with the Objections, to the other House, by which it shall likewise be reconsidered, and if approved by two thirds of that House, it shall become a law. But in all such Cases the Votes of both Houses shall be determined by Yeas and Nays, and the Names of the Persons voting for and against the Bill shall be entered on the Journal of each House respectively. If any Bill shall not be returned by the President within ten Days (Sundays excepted) after it shall have been presented to him, the Same shall be a Law, in like Manner as if he had signed it, unless the Congress by their Adjournment prevent its Return, in which case it shall not be a Law.

Every Order, Resolution, or Vote to which the Concurrence of the Senate and House of Representatives may be necessary (except on a question of Adjournment) shall be presented to the President of the United States; and before the Same shall take Effect, shall be approved by him, or being disapproved by him, shall be repassed by two thirds of the Senate and House of Representatives, according to the Rules and Limitations prescribed in the Case of a Bill.

Section 8. The Congress shall have Power to lay and collect Taxes, Duties, Imposts and Excises, to pay the Debts and provide for the common Defence and general Welfare of the United States; but all Duties, Imposts and Excises shall be uniform throughout the United States;

To borrow Money on the credit of the United States;

To regulate Commerce with foreign Nations, and among the several States, and with the Indian Tribes;

To establish an uniform Rule of Naturalization, and uniform Laws on the subject of Bankruptcies throughout the United States;

To coin Money, regulate the Value thereof, and of foreign Coin, and fix the Standard of Weights and Measures;

To provide for the Punishment of counterfeiting the Securities and current Coin of the United States;

To establish Post Offices and Post Roads;

To promote the Progress of Science and useful Arts, by securing for limited Times to Authors and Inventors the exclusive Right to their respective Writings and Discoveries;

To constitute Tribunals inferior to the supreme Court;

To define and punish Piracies and Felonies committed on the high Seas, and Offenses against the Law of Nations;

To declare War, grant Letters of Marque and Reprisal, and make Rules concerning Captures on Land and Water;

To raise and support Armies, but no Appropriation of Money to that Use shall be for a longer term than two Years;

To provide and maintain a Navy;

To make Rules for the Government and Regulation of the land and naval Forces;

To provide for calling forth the Militia to execute the Laws of the Union, suppress Insurrections and repel Invasions;

To provide for organizing, arming, and disciplining, the Militia, and for governing such Part of them as may be employed in the Service of the United States, reserving to the States respectively, the Appointment of the Officers, and the Authority of training the militia according to the discipline prescribed by Congress;

To exercise exclusive Legislation in all Cases whatsoever, over such District (not exceeding ten Miles square) as may, by Cession of particular States, and the Acceptance of Congress, become the Seat of the Government of the United States, and to exercise like Authority over all Places purchased by the Consent of the Legislature of the State in which the Same shall be, for the Erection of Forts, Magazines, Arsenals, Dockyards, and other needful Buildings;—And

To make all Laws which shall be necessary and proper for carrying into Execution the foregoing Powers, and all other Powers vested by this Constitution in the Government of the United States, or in any Department or Officer thereof.

Section 9. The Migration or Importation of such Persons as any of the States now existing shall think proper to admit, shall not be prohibited by the Congress prior to the Year one thousand eight hundred and eight, but a Tax or Duty may be imposed on such Importation, not exceeding ten dollars for each Person.

The Privilege of the Writ of Habeas Corpus shall not be suspended, unless when in Cases of Rebellion or Invasion the public Safety may require it.

No Bill of Attainder or ex post facto Law shall be passed.

No Capitation, or other direct, Tax shall be laid, unless in Proportion to the Census or Enumeration herein before directed to be taken.

No Tax or Duty shall be laid on Articles exported from any State.

No Preference shall be given by any Regulation of Commerce or Revenue to the Ports of one State over those of another: nor shall Vessels bound to, or from, one State, be obliged to enter, clear, or pay Duties in another.

No Money shall be drawn from the Treasury, but in Consequence of Appropriations made by Law; and a regular Statement and Account of the Receipts and Expenditures of all public Money shall be published from time to time.

No Title of Nobility shall be granted by the United States; and no Person holding any Office of Profit or Trust under them, shall, without the Consent of the Congress, accept of any present, Emolument, Office, or Title, of any kind whatever, from any King, Prince, or foreign State.

Section 10. No State shall enter into any Treaty, Alliance, or Confederation; grant Letters of Marque and Reprisal; coin Money; emit Bills of Credit; make any Thing but gold and silver Coin a Tender in Payment of Debts; pass any Bill of Attainder, ex post facto Law, or Law impairing the Obligation of Contracts, or grant any Title of Nobility.

No State shall, without the Consent of the Congress, lay any Imposts or Duties on Imports or Exports, except what may be absolutely necessary for executing it's inspection Laws: and the net Produce of all Duties and Imposts, laid by any State on Imports or Exports, shall be for the Use of the Treasury of the United States; and all such Laws shall be subject to the Revision and Controul of the Congress.

No State shall, without the Consent of Congress, lay any Duty of Tonnage, keep Troops, or Ships of War in time of Peace, enter into any Agreement or Compact with another State, or with a foreign Power, or engage in War, unless actually invaded, or in such imminent Danger as will not admit of delay.

ARTICLE II

Section 1. The executive Power shall be vested in a President of the United States of America. He shall hold his Office during the Term of four Years, and, together with the Vice President chosen for the same Term, be elected, as follows:

Each State shall appoint, in such Manner as the Legislature thereof may direct, a Number of Electors, equal to the whole Number of Senators and Representatives to which the State may be entitled in the Congress: but no Senator or Representative, or Person holding an Office of Trust or Profit under the United States, shall be appointed an Elector.

The Electors shall meet in their respective States, and vote by Ballot for two Persons, of whom one at least shall not be an Inhabitant of the same State with themselves. And they shall make a List of all the Persons voted for, and of the Number of Votes for each; which List they shall sign and certify, and transmit sealed to the Seat of the Government of the United States, directed to the President of the Senate. The President of the Senate shall, in the Presence of the Senate and House of Representatives, open all the Certificates, and the Votes shall then be counted. The Person having the greatest Number of Votes shall be the President, if such Number be a Majority of the whole Number of Electors appointed; and if there be more than one who have such Majority, and have an equal Number of votes, then the House of Representatives shall immediately chuse by Ballot one of them for President; and if no Person have a Majority, then from the five highest on the List the said House shall in like Manner chuse the

President. But in chusing the President, the Votes shall be taken by States, the Representation from each State having one Vote; a Quorum for this Purpose shall consist of a Member or Members from two thirds of the States, and a Majority of all the States shall be necessary to a Choice. In every Case, after the Choice of the President, the Person having the greatest Number of Votes of the Electors shall be the Vice President. But if there should remain two or more who have equal Votes, the Senate shall chuse from them by Ballot the Vice President.

The Congress may determine the Time of chusing the Electors, and the Day on which they shall give their Votes; which Day shall be the same throughout the United States.

No Person except a natural born Citizen, or a Citizen of the United States, at the time of the Adoption of this Constitution, shall be eligible to the Office of President; neither shall any Person be eligible to that Office who shall not have attained to the Age of thirty five Years, and been fourteen Years a Resident within the United States.

In Case of the Removal of the President from Office, or of his Death, Resignation, or Inability to discharge the Powers and Duties of the said Office, the Same shall devolve on the Vice President, and the Congress may by Law provide for the Case of Removal, Death, Resignation or Inability, both of the President and Vice President, declaring what Officer shall then act as President, and such Officer shall act accordingly, until the Disability be removed, or a President shall be elected.

The President shall, at stated Times, receive for his Services, a Compensation, which shall neither be increased nor diminished during the Period for which he shall have been elected, and he shall not receive within that Period any other Emolument from the United States, or any of them.

Before he enter on the Execution of his Office, he shall take the following Oath or Affirmation:—"I do solemnly swear (or affirm) that I will faithfully execute the Office of President of the United States, and will to the best of my Ability, preserve, protect and defend the Constitution of the United States."

Section 2. The President shall be Commander in Chief of the Army and Navy of the United States, and of the Militia of the several States, when called into the actual Service of the United States; he may require the Opinion, in writing, of the principal Officer in each of the executive Departments, upon any Subject relating to the Duties of their respective Offices, and he shall have Power to grant Reprieves and Pardons for Offenses against the United States, except in Cases of impeachment.

He shall have Power, by and with the Advice and Consent of the Senate, to make Treaties, provided two thirds of the Senators present concur; and he shall nominate, and by and with the Advice and Consent of the Senate, shall appoint Ambassadors, other public Ministers and Consuls, Judges of the supreme Court, and all other Officers of the United States, whose Appointments are not herein otherwise provided for, and which shall be established by Law: but the Congress may by Law vest the Appointment of such inferior Officers, as they think proper, in the President alone, in the Courts of Law, or in the Heads of Departments.

The President shall have Power to fill up all Vacancies that may happen during the Recess of the Senate, by granting Commissions which shall expire at the End of their next session.

Section 3. He shall from time to time give to the Congress Information of the State of the Union, and recommend to their Consideration such Measures as he shall judge necessary and expedient; he may, on extraordinary Occasions, convene both Houses, or either of them, and in Case of Disagreement between them, with Respect to the Time of Adjournment, he may adjourn them to such Time as he shall think proper; he shall receive Ambassadors and other public Ministers; he shall take Care that the Laws be faithfully executed, and shall Commission all the Officers of the United States.

Section 4. The President, Vice President and all civil Officers of the United States, shall be removed from Office on Impeachment for, and Conviction of, Treason, Bribery, or other high Crimes and Misdemeanors.

ARTICLE III

Section 1. The judicial Power of the United States, shall be vested in one supreme Court, and in such inferior Courts as the Congress may from time to time ordain and establish. The Judges, both of the supreme and inferior Courts, shall hold their Offices during good behavior, and shall, at stated Times, receive for their Services, a Compensation, which shall not be diminished during their Continuance in Office.

Section 2. The judicial Power shall extend to all Cases, in Law and Equity, arising under this Constitution, the Laws of the United States, and Treaties made, or which shall be made, under their Authority;—to all Cases affecting Ambassadors, other public Ministers and Consuls;—to all Cases of admiralty and maritime Jurisdiction;—to Controversies to which the United States shall be a Party;—to Controversies between two or more States;—between a State and Citizens of another State;—between Citizens of different States; — between Citizens of the same State claiming Lands under Grants of different States, and between a State, or the Citizens thereof, and foreign States, Citizens or Subjects.

In all cases affecting Ambassadors, other public Ministers and Consuls, and those in which a State shall be Party, the supreme Court shall have original Jurisdiction. In all the other Cases before mentioned, the supreme Court shall have appellate Jurisdiction, both as to Law and Fact, with such Exceptions, and under such Regulations as the Congress shall make.

The Trial of all Crimes, except in Cases of Impeachment, shall be by Jury; and such Trial shall be held in the State where the said Crimes shall have been committed; but when not committed within any State, the Trial shall be at such Place or Places as the Congress may by Law have directed.

Section 3. Treason against the United States, shall consist

only in levying War against them, or in adhering to their Enemies, giving them Aid and Comfort. No Person shall be convicted of Treason unless on the Testimony of two Witnesses to the same overt Act, or on Confession in open Court.

The Congress shall have power to declare the punishment of Treason, but no Attainder of Treason shall work Corruption of Blood, or Forfeiture except during the Life of the Person attainted.

ARTICLE IV

Section 1. Full Faith and Credit shall be given in each State to the public Acts, Records, and judicial Proceedings of every other State. And the Congress may by general Laws prescribe the Manner in which such Acts, Records, and Proceedings shall be proved, and the Effect thereof.

Section 2. The Citizens of each State shall be entitled to all Privileges and Immunities of Citizens in the several States.

A Person charged in any State with Treason, Felony, or other Crime, who shall flee from Justice, and be found in another State, shall on Demand of the executive Authority of the State from which he fled, be delivered up, to be removed to the State having Jurisdiction of the Crime.

No person held to Service or Labor in one State, under the Laws thereof, escaping into another, shall, in Consequence of any Law or Regulation therein, be discharged from such Service or Labor, But shall be delivered up on Claim of the Party to whom such Service or Labor may be due.

Section 3. New States may be admitted by the Congress into this Union; but no new States shall be formed or erected within the Jurisdiction of any other State; nor any State be formed by the Junction of two or more States, or Parts of States, without the Consent of the Legislatures of the States concerned as well as of the Congress.

The Congress shall have Power to dispose of and make all needful Rules and Regulations respecting the Territory or other Property belonging to the United States; and nothing in this Constitution shall be so construed as to Prejudice any

Claims of the United States, or of any particular State.

Section 4. The United States shall guarantee to every State in this Union a Republican Form of Government, and shall protect each of them against Invasion; and on Application of the Legislature, or of the Executive (when the Legislature cannot be convened) against domestic Violence.

ARTICLE V

The Congress, whenever two thirds of both Houses shall deem it necessary, shall propose Amendments to this Constitution, or, on the Application of the Legislatures of two thirds of the several States, shall call a Convention for proposing Amendments, which, in either Case, shall be valid to all Intents and Purposes, as Part of this Constitution, when ratified by the Legislatures of three fourths of the several States, or by Conventions in three fourths thereof, as the one or the other Mode of Ratification may be proposed by the Congress; Provided that no Amendment which may be made prior to the Year one thousand eight hundred and eight shall in any Manner affect the first and fourth Clauses in the ninth Section of the first Article; and that no State, without its Consent, shall be deprived of it's equal Suffrage in the Senate.

ARTICLE VI

All Debts contracted and Engagements entered into, before the Adoption of this Constitution, shall be as valid against the United States under this Constitution, as under the Confederation.

This Constitution, and the Laws of the United States which shall be made in Pursuance thereof; and all Treaties made, or which shall be made, under the Authority of the United States, shall be the supreme Law of the Land; and the Judges in every State shall be bound thereby, any Thing in the Constitution or Laws of any State to the Contrary notwithstanding.

The Senators and Representatives before mentioned, and the Members of the several State Legislatures, and all executive and judicial Officers, both of the United States and of the several States, shall be bound by Oath or Affirmation, to support this Constitution; but no religious Test shall ever be required as a Qualification to any Office or public Trust under the United States.

ARTICLE VII

The Ratification of the Conventions of nine States, shall be sufficient for the Establishment of this Constitution between the States so ratifying the Same.

Done in Convention by the Unanimous Consent of the States present the Seventeenth Day of September in the Year of our Lord one thousand seven hundred and eighty seven and of the Independence of the United States of America the Twelfth. In Witness whereof We have hereunto subscribed our Names,

Go. WASHINGTON—

Presid. and deputy from Virginia

New Hampshire

John Langdon

Nicholas Gilman

Massachusetts

Nathaniel Gorham

Rufus King

Connecticut

Wm. Saml. Johnson

Roger Sherman

New York

Alexander Hamilton

New Jersey

Wil: Livingston

David Brearley

Wm. Paterson

Jona: Dayton

Pennsylvania

B Franklin

Thomas Mifflin

Robt Morris

Geo. Clymer

Thos FitzSimons

Jared Ingersoll

James Wilson

Gouv Morris

Delaware

Geo: Read

Gunning Bedford jun

John Dickinson

Richard Bassett

Jaco: Broom

Maryland

James Mchenry

Dan of St Thos. Jenifer

Danl Carroll

Virginia

John Blair—

James Madison Jr.

North Carolina

Wm. Blount

Rich'd Dobbs Spaight

Hu Williamson

South Carolina

J. Rutledge

Charles Cotesworth Pinckney

Charles Pinckney

Pierce Butler

Georgia

William Few

Abr Baldwin

Attest:

William Jackson, Secretary

The United States Bill of Rights

The Ten Original Amendments
to the Constitution of the United States
Passed by Congress September 25, 1789
Ratified December 15, 1791

I

Congress shall make no law respecting an establishment of religion, or prohibiting the free exercise thereof; or abridging the freedom of speech, or of the press, or the right of the people peaceably to assemble, and to petition the Government for a redress of grievances.

II

A well-regulated militia, being necessary to the security of a free State, the right of the people to keep and bear arms, shall not be infringed.

III

No soldier shall, in time of peace be quartered in any house, without the consent of the owner, nor in time of war, but in a manner to be prescribed by law.

IV

The right of the people to be secure in their persons, houses, papers, and effects, against unreasonable searches and seizures, shall not be violated, and no Warrants shall issue, but upon probable cause, supported by oath or affirmation, and particularly describing the place to be searched, and the persons or things to be seized.

V

No person shall be held to answer for a capital, or otherwise infamous crime, unless on a presentment or indictment of a Grand Jury, except in cases arising in the land or naval forces, or in the Militia, when in actual service in time of War or public danger; nor shall any person be subject for the same offense to be twice put in jeopardy of life or limb; nor shall be compelled in any criminal case to be a witness against himself, nor be deprived of life, liberty, or property, without due process of law; nor shall private property be taken for public use without just compensation.

VI

In all criminal prosecutions, the accused shall enjoy the right to a speedy and public trial, by an impartial jury of the State and district wherein the crime shall have been committed, which district shall have been previously ascertained by law, and to be informed of the nature and cause of the accusation; to be confronted with the witnesses against him; to have compulsory process for obtaining witnesses in his favor, and to have the assistance of counsel for his defense.

VII

In suits at common law, where the value in controversy shall exceed twenty dollars, the right of trial by jury shall be preserved, and no fact tried by a jury shall be otherwise re-examined in any court of the United States, than according to the rules of the common law.

VIII

Excessive bail shall not be required nor excessive fines imposed, nor cruel and unusual punishments inflicted.

IX

The enumeration in the Constitution, of certain rights, shall not be construed to deny or disparage others retained by the people.

X

The powers not delegated to the United States by the Constitution, nor prohibited by it to the States, are reserved to the States respectively, or to the people.

LaVergne, TN USA
11 April 2011
223805LV00005B/80/P

9 781612 030227